THE UPANISHADS

IN THE LIGHT OF KRIYA

LAHIRI MAHASAYA

Paperback: 978-811909034-1

Any references to historical events, real people, or real places are used fictitiously. Names, characters, and places are products of the author's imagination.

Printed by:

Sanage Publishing House LLP
Mumbai, India

sanagepublishing@gmail.com

Shyama Charan Lahiri (30 September 1828 – 26 September 1895), best known as **Lahiri Mahasaya,** was an Indian yogi guru who founded the Kriya Yoga school. In 1861, his non-physical master Mahavatar Babaji appeared to him, ordering him to revive the yogic science of Kriya Yoga to the public after centuries of its guarding by masters.

He became known in the West through Paramahansa Yogananda, a disciple of Sri Yukteswar Giri, and through Yogananda's 1946 book Autobiography of a Yogi, considering him a Yogavatar, or "Incarnation of Yoga," since Lahiri himself was chosen by the yogic masters to disseminate the principles of yoga to the world.

List of Chapters

1 The Dhyanabindu Upanisad : On Meditation   1

2 The Amritabindu Upanishad : On Nectar   17

3 The Niralamba Upanisad   47

4 The Taitiriya Upanisad : On Education   53
     4.1 First Advice   57
     4.2 Second Advice   58
     4.3 Third Advice   62
     4.4 Advice Four   70
     4.5 Advice Five   74
     4.6 Advice Six   80
     4.7 Advice Seven   84
     4.8 Advice Eight   85
     4.9 Advice Nine : On the Adhividya   87
     4.10 Advice Ten   89
     4.11 Advice Eleven   91
     4.12 Advice Twelve   93

5 The Tejabindu Upanisad : The Mystic Energy   95

Chapter 1

The Dhyanabindu Upanisad : On Meditation

**Yogatatiwang prabakshyami Yoginang hitakamaya.
Tat srutwa cha pathitwa cha sarba papai
pramuchyate.**

To remain poised in inner Wisdom steadfastly is the state of Samadhi, that is, attunement with the ultimate Self, which is called Yoga. This attunement is achieved with the help of the five elements : earth, water, fire, air, and ether, or, respectively, the coccygeal, sacral, lumbar, dorsal and cervical centers. This message will benefit those who practice Yoga.

**Visnurnama Mahayogi Mahamayo Mahatapa.
Tatiwa marge jatha dipo drisyate Purusottama.**

Visnu (V+i+u): "Visnu" ordinarily means "Lord Visnu, the Preserver."

V: "bosoms."

I: "firmly tranquilizing the breath up to the aperture in the head (Brahma- randhra) from the eyebrows."

U: "returning to the coccygeal."

Spiritually, "Visnu" is the state of eternal Tranquility at

the After-effect-poise of Kriya.

Mahamaya (Maha+maya):
Maha: "In all beings."
maya: "breathing through the left and right nostril."

Hence, breathing is called *Mahamaya*, because it encompasses all beings, placing them into illusion (Maya).

During the practice of Kriya or at other times when the seeker breaths through the left or right nostril, through the *Ida* (left) or *Pingala* (right) channel of energy, he or she is in illusion.

So long as one's breathing continues, one is in illusion; he will continue to see the world appearance.

When the seeker is able to stop breathing and finds the Tranquil Breath through the left and right nostrils, the breath finds the inner passage of *Susumna*, the Spinal Card, which is the Highway.

Again, when the breath finds the Highway in the Spine, it comes up to the area between the eyebrows and then to the aperture at the top of the head, where it is tranquilized. Only then does the seeker find the Exit from the illusion, or *Maya* (*Ma* : inhaling; *ya* : exhaling), of the whole external manifested world.

In fact, the manifested world is only an illusory appearance due to breathing through the left and the right nostrils.

Therefore, whenever the seeker tranquilizes the subtle air by the practice of *Omkar Kriyas* between the eyebrows and at the aperture in the head, she attains higher dimensions of Consciousness and is in eternal Tranquility. This state of Consciousness is called *Lord Visnu*.

Illumination starts from the very core of Consciousness, that is, the Heart in between the eyebrows, and it goes to the head, or brain, which is the seat of the mind, or restless breath.

There it dissolves the mind, the restless breath, and the intellect, the determining character of the restless breath, and this results in purification of the mind's attachments.

Then it encircles the coccygeal center and comes back to the Heart from where it starts. Thus, the seeker attains the highest state of pure Consciousness, the pure Being.

**Jadi sailasama parang bistirnang jo janan bahuna.
Vidyate dhyanayogen, nanyo veda kadachana.**

By the practice of *1,728* times *Pranayam*, the state of meditation takes place.

Sin, i.e., outward mind from *Brahma*, the ultimate Self, is transcended by that meditation. There is no other means to overcome sin.

When the seeker practices *Pranayam* (or scientific Kriyas) and *Omkar Kriyas* (higher Kriyas of Tranquil Air) about 1,728 times, then the state of meditation takes place. At that time, the seeker's mind is attuned to inward Consciousness leaving outward attention, or sin.

Outward attention of the mind which looks for something with attachment is called sin. The same sin cannot be transcended through outward attention of the mind but only by the turning of the mind away from this world to the inner Self.

**Bijaksharat parang Bindung, Nadang Bindo pare
sthitam.
Susabdanchakshare kshine, nisabdang paramang
padam.**

Brahma is Bija; the ultimate Self, the eternal Source of no decay. Beyond decay is the supreme Being.

When one remains always in Brahma, the ultimate Self, then the subtle atom of the Spot is seen, and Nada, or Omkar, the inner Sound is heard.

Eventually after having seen the divine Spot as the result of listening always to Omkar, the inner Sound, inner Sound and divine Spot vanish. That is the state of the After-effect-poise of Kriya.

Susabda: Omkar, or the inner Sound, loud pitched (udatta), low pitched (anudatta) and quiet (sarita).

After hearing the Sound and seeing the Spot, then eventually there is nothing seen and no sound. That is beyond all. At that state, the Spinal Cord stands erect from the coccygeal to the head.

When the seeker holds onto the Self always, then he sees the divine Spot between the eyebrows and listens to the inner Sound.

By the practice of *Omkar Kriyas* and *Yonimudra* (Beatific Inner Revelation Kriya), he transcends the divine Light, or Spot (Bindu) and inner Sound (Om, or Nada) into the state beyond sound. There, where the Spine is alerted from coccygeal to cerebrum, the eternal Tranquility, or eternal Silence, prevails.

Eternal Silence is unceasing Eloquence

**Anahatancha jachhabdang, tasya sabdasya jatparam.
Tat parang chindayet jastu, sa Yogi chhinna sangsaya.**

One who achieves that soundless state of *Nisabda* beyond *Anahata*, or inner Sound (the sound of a ringing bell, honey-drunken fly, flute, sitar, thunder, roaring, drum, etc.) is a Yogi at the After-effect-poise of Kriya.

At the dorsal center, the Yogi listens to the inner Sound in different forms according to his status of Awareness, and when he goes beyond sound, he is in Silence, i. e., in Tranquility at the After-effect-poise of Kriya. This is the state of pure Consciousness, free from all manifestations.

**Balagra sata sahasrang tasya bhagasya bhagasa.
Tasya bhagasya bhagardhang, tajjneyang
Niranjnanam.**

Whoever can divide the tip of the circumference of a hair into one hundred thousand parts initially with the help of a microscope and then with his mind, can conceptually think of the entire universe as being based on one subtle atom of that part, and can see that atom, thus seeing the Whole. He is absolutely Pure.

When the seeker sees the atom of Consciousness between

the eyebrows after practicing higher Kriyas with the help
of Tranquil Breath, then he attains Knowledge of the absolute Self the state of absolute Perfection free from any
limitations whatsoever.

**Puspa madhye jatha gandhyang, payo madhye jatha
gritam.**
Tila madhye jatha tilang, pasaneswaiba kanchaṇam.

In the rose is the form, or smell, which comes to the
nose to be felt as the roses's smell. The atom of smell
is Brahma, the ultimate Self. In milk is potential butter, which is not visible. Likewise, by the practice of
Pranayam, Brahma, the ultimate Self is realized.

Oil does secrete from mustard seeds unless they are crushed.
Similarly, realization of Brahma, the ultimate Self, is not
possible without the practice of Pranayam. The gold in
stone is only extracted when the knots of the stone are
broken up and the gold is melted by fire.

Likewise, in this physical body made of mud, or gross elements, there are three knots:

1. the tongue,

2. the heart center, and

3. the navel or coccygeal center.

Until these knots are crossed by the practice of Pranayam,
the outward attention of the mind remains stuck hard like
stone. When that state is purified, then the divine Light,
the Light of all lights, the illuminous Self, Brahma is revealed.

As smell is invisible in the rose, butter in the milk, oil in
the seeds, and gold in the stones, so is the ultimate Self,
or formless Consciousness, invisible in the physical body.

To get butter, the milk must be churned. To have oil, the
seeds must be crushed. To have gold, the knots of the
stone must be broken up.

Similarly, the seeker of Truth can only attain eternal Realization of the ultimate Self by crossing the following knots of the physical body:

1. the tongue by the practice of *Khecharimudra,*

2. the heart by the practice of *Pranayam,* or Kriyas, that burn the attachment of the heart with the help of inner Light, and

3. the lumbar center by the practice of *Navi Kriya* in a righteous scientific way.

The ultimate Self is formless and invisible.

Being the ultimate Self rather than seeing the ultimate Self is eternal Realization. Being means Existence and Consciousness.

The ultimate Self which is formless, sees no forms. The ultimate Self is formless and wordless.

Ebang sarbani bhutani, manisutramibatmani.
Sthira buddhir sangmuro, Brahmabid Brahmani
sthita.

Thus, all the living and non-living beings are individuals on one string which is the string of the Cause of all beings who is the ultimate Self.

Like the binding string of the peral necklace, the ultimate Self is in the individual [in the physical body], and He ties all living and non-living beings.

When the intellect is poised perfectly in Tranquility, this is the state of the After-effect-poise of Kriya. Here Sound can be known. This is the state of the Knower of Brahma.

The Knowledge of Brahma is to know Brahma. In this state, one is attuned in Oneness with Him, the ultimate Self, Purna Brahma, at the state of After-effect-poise of Kriya.

The ultimate Self being the ultimate Existence, is in all living and non-living beings as a connecting string. The seeker can realize Oneness with the ultimate Self at the After-effect-poise of Kriya through the Tranquil Breath by the practice of scientific Kriyas.

**Tilanantu jatha tailang puspe gandhamibarpitam.
Purusasya sarire tu, sa bajyabhyantare sthita.**

The oil of the mustard seed is extracted only when the mustard seed is crushed. The fragrance has always been in the flower, but the atom brings it out.

Similarly, in the physical body resides Brahma, the ultimate Self. With the practice of Kriya He can be seen outside as well.

It is the first duty of a seeker to realize the ultimate Self inside through deeper Kriya practice; then, the same Self can be seen outside (as the outside is a reflection of the inside).

**Brikshantu sakalang Bidyachhaya, tasyaiba Niskala.
Sakale Niskale bhabe, sarbatratma byabasthita.**

Respiration in the physical body can be likened to an upside-down tree: the roots are at the head and the branches and leaves are below. Know it very well. Manifestation is a shadow and reflection of the same tree: In other words, the tree of life has become *Niskala* by the light of the ultimate Self.

Sakala: There is a supreme Being beyond the three qualities inside the physical body with his own vibrations. He is the Tranquil Self at the After-effect-poise of Kriya. He is perfectly present in all beings.

Niskala: A state where the air outside the body remains outside, *Prana* [upward life force] and *Apana* [downward life force] are balanced, and air flows inside the nostril. When such a state is held, it is the sign of Samadhi, i.e., the state of Attunement with the ultimate Self. Then the Self is everywhere.

When the seeker attains the tranquil Breath by the practice of Pranayam, or Kriya, then the Prana, or the upward life force, and Apana, or the downward life force, is balanced, or at the Equilibrium state.

So air on the outside remains outside, as Apana, or downward life force, which is entrusted to drag air inside in equilibrium. For the same reason, the air inside the body cannot go outside because the Prana, or upward life force, is in equilibrium and tranquil.

So the air inside the body, being Tranquil Air, will function in a subtle way, continuing to flow just inside the nostril. This is the state of Samadhi, or attunement in Oneness.

The state is called *Niskala*, while *Sakala* means that the supreme Being is beyond three qualities at the After-effect-poise of Kriya and is Tranquil everywhere.

The Self is all-pervading within (Sakala) and without (Niskala) and is beyond.

**Atasi puspa sankasang, navi sthane pratisthitam.
Chaturvujang Mahabirang puraken bichintayet.**

Like a petaled flower is the four-armed form of almighty Lord Mahadev, the Great Lord, to be remembered during inhaling.

During inhaling while practicing Kriya, the seeker must remember the great, radiant, energetic Lord Mahadev in the navel, i. e., at the lumbar center, to awaken towards inner Realization.

**Kumbhaken hridisthane, chintayet Kamalasanam.
Brahmanang raktagourang, chaturvaktam
Pitamaham.**

By *Kumbhak*, i.e., *Kebala Kumbhaka*, in other words, by help of the tranquil state of the air of respiration which is naturally held during the practice of *Pranayam*, the Self is revealed in the dorsal center.

Practicing Kriya around four sides of red fire, the seeker is to see *Kutastha* in between the eyebrows through *Yonimudra*.

That very state when the air of breathing becomes tranquil during the practice of Kriya is called *Kumbhaka*. There are two types of Kumbhaka:

1. Sahita, and

2. Kebala.

Sahita means "with the help of " Stopping breathing with the help of Sahita, or artificial intention, using force, either holding the air outside or inside the body, is called "Sahita Kumbhaka. "

Kebala means "simply" or "naturally." That very state when the air of breathing becomes automatically Tranquil during practice of Kriya without using any force or intention to stop it is called "Kebala Kumbhaka. "

Kebala Kumbhaka places the seeker into spontaneous practice, and personal efforts drop off automatically. It may be mentioned here that the Kriya Yoga science supports the system of Kebala Kumbhaka.

Sahit Kumbhaka is a bit dangerous for the person who is suffering from heart disease while the Kebala Kumbhaka is free from such potentially fatal complications, as breath switches over to spontaneity naturally.

The verse explains that the same mystic Energy of the lumbar center, at the dorsal center, becomes more powerful and appears like red flaming fire. At that time, the seeker practices higher Kriyas like Omkar Kriyas, Cosmo-electro-magnetizing or Transmigrating Kriyas, into Oneness, and sees the inner Self, or Kutastha, between the eyebrows by the practice of Yonimudra.

**Rechaken tu Bidyatma, lalatastahng Trilochanam.
Suddha sphatika sangkasang, Niskalang papnasanam.**

By exhaling and putting the breath in the self and, at the same time, by raising the tongue towards the head, the seeker will see in Kutastha the great Lord Mahadev who appears like a dazzling white light in between the eyebrows.

Niskalang: This dazzling Light destroys the outward attention of the mind, that is, all sins. The seeker shall have to cross through these three knots by the practice of Kriya, which can be known personally from the Guru.

When the seeker tranquilizes the breath by means of exhaling and puts it between the eyebrows and applies the Khecharimudra to send the tongue towards the head, then, he sees the inner Self who is the Lord of all gods in Kutastha, that is, in between the eyebrows, in dazzling inner Light.

This Light attracts the mind towards the Lord to destroy outward attention of the mind, which is sin. Outward attention of the mind, looking for outward things, is called attachment, or sin. This is the root of all troubles in everybody's life.

When this root is eradicated by seeing the inner Self between the eyebrows in the inner Light in the inner Body, i.e., the subtle body, then the three knots are removed. Then all doubts and confusions of the seeker about the ultimate Self are dispelled.

**Astapatramadha puspamurdhanalamadhomukham.
Kadali puspa sankasang, sarbadevamayatmakam.**

All gods are stuck in the Atma, or self, in between the eyebrows. It is like in the flower of a banana. [From the navel, at the eight-petaled lumber center, the downward stem of the lotus is upside to the heart up to Brahmarandhra, the aperture of the head].

At the navel, or lumbar center, the closed downward facing eight-petalled lotus turns upward and its stem moves towards the dorsal center up to the aperture of Brahma in the head by the practice of Navi Kriya and Kriya, or Pranayam.

The individual energy finds its high Way upward inside the Spinal Cord.

The reflection can be seen in between the eyebrows, an area which acts as a radar to reveal inner Beatific refined happenings.

It appears like a banana flower where all the gods, or countless numbers of realized saints and sages, are in condensed form in a small space in the inner Self in between the eyebrows.

Satabjang satapatradyang, biprakimabja karnikam.
Tatrarka chandra banhinamu parjupari chintayet.

The inner Self is in the whole universe in the form of Kutastha. The entire universe is from the lumbar to the dorsal, from the dorsal to the cervical, from the cervical to the medulla oblongata, and from the medulla oblongata to the thousand petals.

When the seeker arrives there, first he sees what resembles fire, then it appears as though a hundred thousand suns were dazzling in the Sky.

In the center, millions of billions of dazzling gods, sages, realized ones and seers are seen eternally present before Kutastha, the inner Self.

Arriving there and gradually thinking of [meditating on] the inner Self, the seeker achieves the state of satisfaction.

Gradually and eventually the seeker finds the inward Highway through the Spinal Cord which passes through the lumbar, dorsal and cervical centers, the medulla oblongata and in between the eyebrows to the thousand petalled cerebrum to attain the eternal state of Contentment and absolute Freedom.

He happens to observe a dazzling bright inner Light and in the center, before 38 The Upanisads the inner Self, millions of billions of gods, sages, seers, saints and realized souls are eternally present there in between the eyebrows.

Padmasyosthapanang krittva, borung chandragni
surjayo.
Tasyahurbbijamahritya, Atma sancharate Dhrubam.

Thus having raised the lotus to the dazzling light of the moon and sun, seeing the seed, i.e., Brahma, the ultimate Self, the seeking self is poised perfectly in Oneness with the ultimate Self.

When the seeker finds the inner Way to cross through the centers, i. e., lotuses in the Spinal Card by the practice of Kriya, very soon he enters into Oneness with the pure Sel, which is the seed, or Source, of all.

Tristhanancha Trimargancha, Tribrahma cha Triraksharam.
Trimatranchardhamatrancha, jastang Veda sa Vedabit.

One who knows the following knows perfectly knowing, or Knowledge, i.e., the After-effect-poise of Kriya. In other words, he understands, or realizes, Himself.

Three places: coccygeal, dorsal and the area between the eyebrows (Bhu, Bhuba, and Swa),

Three paths: Ida, Pingala and Susunma [Spinal Cord],

Three Brahma: Sunya Brahma [Void Self], Kutastha Brahma [inner Self] and Brahma [the ultimate Self at the After-effect-poise of Kriya].

Three letters: *A U M*, Creator, Sustainer and Absorber [Brahma, Visnu and Maheswar],

Three points and a half: Navel, Heart, Throat and a half point:

Brahma, or the ultimate Self, is ever Tranquil from the throat to between the eyebrows.

When the seeker of Truth through deeper Kriya practice overcomes the Trinity, i. e., manifestation, awareness, and dissolution, then he is in the higher dimension of awareness of Consciousness.

Even in this state of dualism, he has to be dissolved through inner Sound.

Then he realizes the perfect state of Oneself i.e., the absolute state of Knowledge which includes all.

Tailadharamibachhinnang, dirgha ghanta ninadabat.
Abagajang Pranavasyagrang, jastang Veda sa Veadabit.

Omkar, or inner Sound, is continuous, like the pouring of oil from a container high up. That continuous inner Sound is like a continuous ringing bell.

Abagajang: it is not possible to know this inner Sound, OM (Aum), from speech.

Pranavading: one who knows the place of that inner Sound is practically dissolved and is the Knower of the Vedas. That is, he knows knowing at the After-effect-poise of Kriya.

OM (Aum), or inner Sound, is continuous like the sound of ringing bells.

It is revealed when the seeker is in a higher state of Consciousness resulting from the practice of Omkar Kriya.

This inner Sound is dissolved in the very Source of all, i. e., Brahma, or the ultimate Self at the After-effect-poise of Kriya.

Pranavo dhanu sarojyatma, Brahma
tallakshyamuchyate.
Apramattven Vedhabyang sarabattanmato bhabet.

If the inner Sound, OM, is heard by the practice of Kriya while the body is living, then it is dissolved in Brahma, the ultimate Self. Thereby, all become the ultimate Self. When everything becomes the ultimate Self, then all is done.

When the seeker listens to the inner Sound, OM, by the practice of Omkar Kriyas, which are higher Kriyas of Tranquil Air, and dissolves this sound in the ultimate Self, then everything is dissolved in the ultimate Self.

When everything becomes the Self the seeker attains Oneness with the Pure Self This is the highest Attainment, or eternal Realization.

Swadehamaraning krittva. Pranavanchottaranim.
Dhyananirmanthanavyasadevang, pasyennigurahbat.

Treat this physical body as one dry wood and the inner Sound, OM (that is automatically heard), as another dry wood.

Thereafter, by the practice of Pranayam 1,728 times, you will see the secret inner Self and then loose the power of speaking.

The seeker is advised in this verse to treat the physical body as if it were one dry wood stick and the inner Sound, OM, as if it were another dry wood stick being agitated with friction to produce fire; in this case, to produce the mystic Energy or Light with the practice of Pranayam (Omkar Kriya)1,728 times and in that Inner Light to see the Inner Self.

This is the most secret science.

When the seeker realizes the inner Self in the inner Light produced by the practice of Pranayama, or Kriya of Tranquil Air, he realizes the ultimate Self.

Thereby, he becomes silent simply because his intellect is dissolved and poised in inner Wisdom. This silence is not the silence of speech, but the silence of mind or thoughts.

Eternal Realization is beyond thoughts and intellect.

Jathaibotpalanalen, toyamarkasayet puna.
Tathaibotkarsayedwayung, Yogi yoga pade sthita.

As water is dragged up through the stem of a flower from the roots, likewise, the seeker shall have to inhale air through the Spinal Cord from the coccygeal center and exhale according to the instructions he has received personally from his Guru.

Thus, whoever enters into spontaneous Oneness with the ultimate Self (Samadhi) by practicing Kriya 20,736 times regenerates the eternal exalted Consciousness.

The seeker must practice Pranayam, or Kriya, according to instructions received personally from the Guru, or Master.

He will have to dive deeper into Kriya to practice 20,736 times.

Thus, finally, he can enter into spontaneous Oneness with

the ultimate Self This is called the highest Attainment, or eternal Tranquility, or Peace.

Ardhamatrang rajjung kritwa, kupa bhutantu pankajam.
Karsayennalamargena, Bhrubormadhye nayellayam.

Think of the air as a rope operating between the throat and the eyebrows to attract the air which operates down below in the well in the centers (throat, dorsal, navel, sacral, and coccygeal) of the five elements, dissolving them in the area between the eyebrows, i.e., at the *Ajna* center at *Kutastha*.

As people drag water from the well with the help of a rope and bucket, similarly, with the help of Tranquil Air operating between the eyebrows and throat, the seeker must bring up the air operating in the five elements in the lower centers (throat, dorsal, lumbar, sacral and coccygeal) and dissolve it between the eyebrows in the *Ajna* center in *Kutastha*, the inner Self.

Only then can the seeker enter into Oneness with the pure Consciousness of the ultimate Self, dissolving dualism, i.e., the individuality of his or her own, to attain infinite Bliss.

Bhrubormadhye lalatastu, nasikayantu mulata.
Amritasthanang bijaniyadwiswasyayatanang mahat.
Biswasyayatanang mahaditi.

In between the eyebrows, at the root of the nose in the forehead, is the place of nectar. Whoever stays there is eternal and all-pervading and, therefore, is great.

In this verse, it is mentioned that whoever stays in between the eyebrows is all-pervading and, therefore, is great and undecaying.

When the seeker practices *Talabya Kriya*, or *Khecharimudra*, successfully, then the tip of the tongue arrives between the eyebrows to the root of the nose in the forehead. Then he must touch the place of nectar according to the advice of his Master, or Guru.

Thereby, he attains the higher dimension of Consciousness.

This places him in the universal stand as all-pervading and great.

The practice of *Talabya Kriya* provides him with the capacity to come out from the physical body to remove obstacles within and without into Oneness in order to attain the ultimate Self.

OM. Shanti! Shanti! Shanti!

Chapter 2

The Amritabindu Upanishad : On Nectar

In the *Atharva Veda*, twenty-two verses of the *Amrita Bindu Upanishad* are referred to as the *Amrita Nada Upanisad*.

Om Paramatmane namaha

("Bowing to the ultimate Self")

**Sastranyadhito medhabi, avyasya cha puna puna.
Paramang Brahma bidyaya, ulkabannanyatho srijet.**

Sastra: the substance of all scriptures is Kriya, or practice.

adhitya: dissolve the intellect.

medhabi: by looking at the atom of Brahma, or the ultimate Self, the past, future and present and all who are in Brahma can be known.

avyasya: after practicing again and again.

Paramang: after everything at the After-effect-poise of Kriya, the ultimate Self is realized.

ulkaban: like a falling star.

na anyatha: the mind will not go outward.

utsrilet: will not take away.

The substance of all scriptures is the practice of Kriya which results in the dissolution of the intellect poising the seeker in inner Wisdom by which he attains Eternity (past, present, and future).

The steadfast practice of Kriya gradually brings the seeker to the After-effect-poise of Kriya where his seeking self is merged in Brahma, the ultimate Self.

> **Omkarang rathalnarujyang, Visunung krittva tu sarathim.**
> **Brahmaloka padanwesi, Rudraradhana tatpara.**

Omkara: The physical body is like a chariot having six centers as wheels.

Visnu: The After-effect-poise of Kriya, that is, Visnu, is to be taken as a charioteer [guide, or Guru] to whom the seeker can inquire about what is inside the body at the After-effect-poise of Kriya in the ultimate Self.

Rudra: putting the mind into *Kutastha*, the inner Self.

aradhana: Thinking.

A: Visnu, or steadfastness in the coccygeal center.

ra: taking the mind from the coccygeal center to the eye.

dha: achieving steadfast tranquility by dissolution of the intellect.

na: thus being tranquilized, the seeker continues to see at the tip of the nose.

The verse indicates how to practice Kriya in the physical body, which is like a chariot having six wheels.

Through the practice of *Omkar Kriyas* at the After-effect-poise of Kriya the seeker achieves eternal Tranquility, which is the guide for the seeker to inquire about and realize the state of ultimate Existence.

The seeker must make the mind inward by the practice of Kriya and put this inward focus of mind into *Kutastha* to move inwardly from the coccygeal center to high up between the eyebrows where the intellect is dissolved. Thus poised in inner Wisdom, the seeker now has the higher dimension to receive higher Consciousness and to see the beatific inner Revelations, or visions, between the eyebrows.

Tabadrathen gantabayang, jabadratha pathi sthita.
Chhittva ratha patha sthanang, rathamutsrijya
gachhati.

The seeker should practice *Pranayam* of the six centers as long as he finds the way. When the way is finished, then he should renounce the Kriya; that is, movement in the Tranquil Air is inexplicable.

The seeker must practice Kriya as long as he can go through the inward way to the higher dimension.

When he arrives at the end of the path, then he shall have to switch over to the Tranquil Breath, which is by itself inexplicable in nature.

That is, when the seeker finds the Tranquil Air of respiration, he should renounce Kriya to switch over to the tranquil state of Air to hold on to the spontaneous state of natural Bliss Awareness which is the inexplicable way to absolute Freedom.

Matra lingapadang takttva, sabda banjana barjita.
Aswaren makaren padang sukshmancha gachhati.

The After-effect-poise of Kriya is that state where there is no earth, water, fire, air or ether at all. There is no linga, or sign; neither is there Sound.

That is, there is neither the inner Sound, OM, nor the sound of respiration. This state is beyond respiration.

M: Manibandha, i.e., *Kutastha*, the inner Self is not there, i.e., appearing like *Kutastha* is an atom in the central point having very subtle resonating vibrations.

All are dissolved: the atom of earth in the atom of water, the atom of water in the atom of fire, the atom of fire in the atom of air, the atom of air in the atom of ether and the atom of ether in the atom of Brahma, or the ultimate

Self. And in one part of the atom of the ultimate Self, the whole world rests and goes to such a subtle state.

The state of After-effect-poise of Kriya is so subtle that there is no vibration of the five elements, neither sound of respiration, nor even inner Sound: Nada, or OM. It is beyond all. Even *Kutastha*, the inner Self, is not there.

It is just one pure Equilibrium, Harmonious State of Consciousness: in other words, it is the eternally Tranquil State of Silence, poised in Peace.

**Sabdadi bisaya pancha, manaschaibatichanchalam.
Chintayedatmano rasmin, pratyahara sa uchyate.**

First, everything is heard through the sound of words; then visions are seen through the sound. Smell is received through the sound. Taste is felt through the sound. The sound is known through the sound.

Sabda (Sound): *Sa* (Lord Siva) + *b* (throat) + *da* (being attracted up to the coccygeal center).

Attractions [practicing *Omkar Kriyas*] within the body produce sounds through which understanding is reached. This is called "sound."

Bisaya pancha (the five means): there are five means, or doors, by which it is felt:

1. Chaksu (eye)

2. Jioha (tongue),

3. Nasika (nose),

4. Tvaka (skin), and

5. Kama (ear).

Manaschaibati chanchalam

Mana (Mind): the restless individual soul is the mind upon which one should think [meditate].

Chintayedatmano rasmin

: By constant thinking [meditation], there will will be knowledge of the Self [Atma] or eventually one will see the rays of inner Realization, i.e., step to the secret science from which all forms of inner Revelations are seen and where there is no moon, sun or radiations of fire.

Once arriving there, the mind does not return. This is called inwardness, or *Pratyahara*, i.e., interiorization, meaning stoppage of restless movement of the mind toward outwardness.

The whole sense world is made of sound. All the five senses receive worldly awareness by means of sound. When by the Practice Of Kriya some sound is concentrated, inner Realization is revealed.

Inner Light then reveals the inner beatific visions, or Revelations, which are beyond the sun, moon and fire. This inward state of sensation is called *Pratyahara*, and from it the mind practically cannot go outward. This inwardness is the means to inner Life, or eternal Realization.

Pratyaharastatha dhyanang, Pranayamojatha dharana.
Tarkaschaiba samashischa, sarango Yoga uchyatae.

Pranayam is the state of Tranquility between inhaling and exhaling.

By the practice of twelve (12) pranayams, pratyahara is held. By the practice of 144 Pranayams, Dharana, or concept, is formed. By 1,728 Pranayams, Dhyana, or meditation, is held.

Tranquilizing breathing at the coccygeal center, bringing the tranquilized breath between the eyebrows and sending it to the head to contemplate there is *tarka*, dissolving the intellect.

By the practice of 20,736 Pranayams, Samadhi, or attunement in Oneness, is attained. This is called the six-steps Yoga.

The tranquil state of breathing in a natural way by the practice of inhaling and exhaling is called *Pranayam*, and by 12 Pranayams, Pratyahara, the state of inwardness, is attained.

Again, by the practice of 144 Pranayams, the tree Dharana, or glimpses of the equilibrium state of Consciousness, or Self, is formed. Then by the practice of 1,728 Pranayams, the state of meditation, or Dhyana, is achieved.

When at that state the intellect is dissolved, or poised in inner Wisdom, then by the practice of 20,736 Pranayams, Samadhi, or attunement in Oneness between the seeking Self and ultimate Self, is attained. This is called "six-fold Yoga."

**Jatha parvatadhatunang, dajyate dhamanammala.
Tathendriya krittva dosa, dajyante Prana nigrahat.**

As all dust of *dhatus* [metals] of a mountain melt when burnt by heavy fire. Likewise, the impurities of mind are burnt by the practice of Kriya through inhaling and exhaling.

All things are burnt to ashes. The defect of senses, i.e., outward attention of the mind, is burnt by tranquilizing *Prana* by the practice of Kriya.

That is, Kriya practice is the only means to destroy outward attention of the mind. The attachment, outward attention of the mind, is the root of all the troubles of life situations. That attachment is burnt to ashes by the practice of Kriya by means of inhaling and exhaling.

Sincere Kriya practice is the only way to destroy that root of attachment or outward attention. When the mind is made inward, outward attention is destroyed.

**Pranayamoirddaheddosan, dharanavischa kilwisim.
Kilwisancha kshayang nitwa, ruchiranchaiba
chintayet.**

Dosa: Putting the attention of the mind away from Brahma, the ultimate Self, is the defect.

Pranayamoirddahe: By the practice of *Pranayam*, that defect of being outward is destroyed automatically.

dharanavischa: By the practice of 144 Pranayams, Dharana [concept] is held.

Kilwisa: When the intellect is forced by effort to hold onto the head (Tranquility) and by that determined intellect some wrong is done or said which results in sin, automatically one suffers internally as though he were poisoned. That suffering is removed by the practice of 144 Pranayams. Thus, the practice of 144 Pranayams everyday destroys the suffering of the mind.

Ruchira: *R* (eye or energy) + *U* (coccygeal); again from the eye to the coccygeal center, that is, to inhale Kriya again.

Chirang: to think always, i.e., to practice Kriya always.

The outward attention of the mind which is sin can be destroyed by the practice of Pranayam. Even the painful suffering of the mind can be destroyed by the practice of 144 Pranayams everyday.

The seeker is advised to practice Kriya from the eyebrows to the coccygeal center again and again.

Ruchire rechaka nchaiba, bayorakarsanantatha.
Pranayamastraya praokta, rechaka puraka kumbhaka.

Ruchira explained above, again is mentioned here clearly. When exhaling extends to the coccygeal center, inhaling automatically starts again. That is, automatically air is attracted. Thus, practicing inhaling and exhaling, automatically *Kumbhaka* [Tranquil Breath] is held. These three are named as *Pranayam*.

By the sincere practice of inhaling and exhaling, automatically *Kumbhaka*, the Tranquil state of Air, is attained in natural course.

This is called *Kebala*, or *Kumbhaka*, the state of Tranquility which is attained in the natural course of Kriya practice without using artificial force or intention to hold the air of the breath inside or outside the body. This is *Pranayam*.

Sabyabahriti sapranavang, Gayitring sirasa saha.
Tri pathedayat Prana Pramayam sa uchyate.

The six centers and apertures of Brahma (*Brahmarandhra*) are the seven *Brahriti*, or "states of vibration."

1. Om,

2. Bhu,

3. Swa,

4. Maha,

5. Jana,

6. Tapa, and

7. Satya

The seeker is advised to practice *Gayatri Omkar Kriya* with the body of *Pranava (Nada)*. After practicing *Pranayam* up to the head, practice *Omkar Kriya* three times and focus *Prana* in each center according to the advice received personally from the *Guru*. This is called *Pranayam*. The verse deals with how the Pranayam is to be practiced with the Tranquil Air, or Breath, with the help of *Gayatri Omkar Kriya* up to the head.

The tranquilization of Breath between the throat and eyebrows is *Gayatri* in the Kriya Light. In the Veda, *Gayatri* means "Divine Mother," *the mystic Energy.* To attain that Energy, there is a particular Mantra practiced during *Pranayam* which stands as follows:

Om Bhur Bhuba Swa Tat Sabitur barenang bhargo Devasya dhimahi. Dhiyo yona prochodayat

The same is achieved by the *Omkar Kriyas.* The *Omkar Kriya*: are to be practiced three times at every center according to the instructions received personally from the Master, or Guru. This is called *Pranayam.*

Utkshipya bayitmakasang, sunya krittva niratmakam.
Sunya bhaben Yumjiyadrekasyeti lakshanam.

Throwing the air into the sky, holding onto the After-effect-poise of Kriya, holding onto the ultimate Self (Brahma) alone and holding the breath on Brahma, one should practice Kriya. By this, *Rechaka* will be held. In other words, the seeker will remain Tranquil.

Extracting the breath to the outside and holding onto Tranquility at the After-effect-poise of Kriya, the seeker is advised to hold the Tranquil Breath onto the self thereby, causing *Rechaka* (exhaling) to hold onto the Tranquil state of Air to generate Tranquility.

**Na chochhaswennanuchhasennoi gatrani chalayet.
Ebang bayurgrahitabya, purakasyeti lakshanam.**

When the body expels wind, or is yawning, the seeker must not practice *Pranayam*. *Pranayam* is to be practiced with the body erect. Accepting air in such way is called *Puraka*.

The seeker is advised to practice Kriya with the body and Spine erect and not to practice Kriya while the body expels wind, or is yawning. Taking the air inside is called inhaling, or *Puraka*.

**Baktronotpalanalena, bayung krittva nirasrayam.
Ebang bayurgrahitabya, Kumbhakasyeti lakshanam.**

When the breath is detached from its object, i.e, made Tranquil as though sucking through the Spinal Cord path like the stem of a lily, it is automatically tranquilized. This is the sign of *Kumbhaka*, or Tranquility. That is, when the air flows in and out in the Spinal Cord tranquilly, it is the state of *Kumbhaka*, Tranquility. As a man sucks water from a glass with the help of the stem of a lily or lotus flower, likewise, the seeker should drag air through the Spinal Cord from the bottom of the Spine, i.e., from the coccygeal center, making the air free from manifestation and tranquilizing the breath. In the tranquil state of air, subtle air flows tranquilly and automatically in and out of the Spinal Cord. This is the state of *Kebali Kumbhaka* where the air of respiration is tranquil in a natural way when it enters the Spine.

Andhabat pasya rupani, srinu sabdamakarnabat.
Kasthabat pasyate dehang, prasantsyati lakshanam.

Andhabat (like the blind): As the blind see forms, likewise, the seeker is advised to see the forms. He does not hear with his ears, yet sound [*Omkar*] is heard inside like a kind of listening by the deaf. The body is like dry wood. When the seeker is not in the house [body], that is, when there is no individual existence, he achieves some tranquility.

When the seeker attains the state of After-effect-poise of Kriya, he achieves the perfect state of awareness of *I am nothing and I have nothing*. When the seeker attains the tranquil state at the After-effect-poise of Kriya, then the physical body dies and the senses do not act; yet he sees and hears inside.

Then, he is established in the awareness that *I am nothing and I have nothing*. This leads him to attain eternal Tranquility.

Mana sankalpakang dhyatwa, sangkshipyatmani
buddhiman.
Dharayitwa tathatmanang, dharana parikirtita.

Perfectly dissolving all future desires in the Self when there is no thought and when 144 times *Pranayam* is practiced is called concept, or *dharana*. When the seeker dissolves all future desires in the Self, then there is no more thought. At that time, if the seeker practices 144 times *Pranayams*, or Kriyas, he can have a true concept of life, or the Self, in the state beyond desires.

This very state is called *Dharana*, or a glimpse of the equilibrium State, or Concept. The true Concept of ultimate Tranquility is possible only when one attains the state beyond thoughts.

Agamasyabirodhen, uhanang tarka ucyate.
Jang labdhdpyabamanyeta, samadhi parikirtita.

Agamasyabirodhen: incoming; having no obstruction to the incoming breath. In other words, the air of respiration comes and goes in a subtle way through the Spinal Cord.

Uhanang: *U* (steadfast tranquility at the coccygeal center) + *ha* (the upward movement of *Pranbayu*, the life force) + *na* (the upward movement of respiration from the nose called dissolving *tarka*, the intellect).

In other words, attaining the After-effect-poise of Kriya and attuning the mind with Tranquility, or the equilibrium state, which is called *Samadhi*. When there is no obstruction to the air of respiration flowing in and out through the Spinal Cord in a subtle way, then the intellect dissolves into inner Wisdom at the After-effect-poise of Kriya. This is called *Samadhi*, or the equilibrium State of intellect in a poised state. This leads to eternal Tranquility, or eternal Peace.

Bhumi bhage same ramye, sarbadosabibarjit.
Krittva manomaying rakshang, japta chaibatha
mandalam.

Attaining the state of inwardness, one realizes the ultimate Self by holding onto *Sthiti*(Tranquility) at the earth, or coccygeal center, i.e., not putting the mind away, but keeping the mind within the mind [dissolving the mind in the Source of mind]. That is the state of *Brahmamay*, or Oneness with the ultimate Self.

The seeker is advised to dissolve the mind in the innermost point of the mind itself and to attain eternal Tranquility, thereby realizing the ultimate Self.

Padmakang swaswtikang byapi, bhadrasanamathapi.
Baddha Yogasanang samyaguttaravimukha sthita.

Practice *Pranayam* sitting either in *Padmasan*(the lotus posture), *swaswatika, bhadrasan, baddha padmasan* (the half-lotus posture), or in *Yogasan*, facing north.

The seeker is advised to sit in a particular posture with one-pointed steadfastness of mind channelized upward inside the Spinal Card. This is how Kriya should be practiced.

Nasika putamangulya, pidhaiken marutam.
Akrisya dharayedgning, sabdamebavichintayet.

Inhaling one time through the nostril and holding [the
state of being poised], one should think of the seven spread-
ings (*Brahriti*).

This verse deals with the procedure of practice. The seeker
is advised to inhale through the nostril; holding the tranquil state of air of breathing, he is to practice Kriya strictly
in accordance with the instructions he has received personally from his Guru.

Omiteksharang Brahma, Omityeken rechayet.
Divya Mantren bahusa, kurjyadatmamala chyutim.

Fill up with *Omkar* and exhale with *Omkar Mantra*.
Practice gradually again and again. The impurities of the
Self, i.e., outward attention of the mind, will not remain.
This is the state of Kriya.

This verse deals with the practice of *Omkar Kriya*, which
is a higher Kriya of the tranquil Breath. The seeker is
advised to inhale according to the advice he has received
personally from his *Gurudev* to practice the *Omkar Kriya*
with a particular Mantra of *OM*. When he practices these
Omkar Kriyas for receiving higher Consciousness again
and again, then all his impurities, that is, outward attention of the mind, are destroyed. The mind then dissolves
in its Source, and the seeker merges in the spontaneous
state.

Paschadhyayet purboktang, kramanmantrang
binirddiset.
Stulatisthulamatrayang, nati murdhamatikrama.

As advised before, hold onto the back with the sound
of *OM*. You should not exhale or inhale more. The verse
indicates that the seeker practice *Omkar Kriya* with the
particular OM Mantra on the backside (the Spine) as advised by the Guru. The seeker should not continue to
breathe in and out more.

**Tirjagurdhamadhya dristing, binirdharjya Mahamati.
Sthirasthayi biniskampastada Yogang samavyaset.**

When the sight is above and below, then automatically the concept is known, that is, can be known, from the mouth of the Guru (*Guru-vakta-gamya*).

Being so tranquil, the seeker should practice Yoga, i.e., *Dharana-Dhyana-Samadhi* [concept-meditation-attunement].

When the seeker tranquilizes breath, his sight gazes above and below. Then automatically he attains the true concept of Tranquility (peace) in life. At this tranquil Breath, he must practice Yoga or Kriya with true *Dharana-Dhyan-Samadhi*: respectively, concept, meditation and attunement.

Lahiri Mahasay makes it abundantly clear that the instructions for the practice of this Pranayam must be received directly from "the mouth of the Guru."

**Talamtra tatha Yogo, dharana yoajanantatha.
Dwadasamatro Yogastu, kalato niyata smrita.**

Talukshan: one second, or that fraction of time which passes during the clapping of hands. This is the state of the subtle body of the five elements (*Pancho-tanmatra*). At that state, the Tranquility of Lord Visnu generates at the soft palate and spreads throughout the body through the nerves, arteries and Spinal Cord.

The rhythms by which it [the manifestations of vibrations of Consciousness] is being felt in all the nerves throughout the body reveals the form of the second which is being felt by the touch of all the external senses.

But it is not possible to feel the inner Awareness by the external senses. This is only possible through the deeper states of Kriya, or Yoga [Oneness, or Union, with the ultimate Self].

The practice of twelve (12) Pranayams, or Kriyas, constitute one *Pratyahara* (inwardness).

The practice of 144 Pranayams makes one Dharana (concept); the practice of 1,728 Pranayams makes Dhyana (meditation); and the practice of 20,736 Pranayams makes Samadhi (Oneness- Attunement).

The steadfast state of this Oneness-Attunement is called Yoga. To remain attuned at the After-effect-poise of Kriya is *Yojan.*

If the yogi practices 12 times (samadhi), he can triumph over the influence of death, and he shall not have to face death. This can be known personally from the mouth of the Guru.

The verse deals with how the seeker can overcome death and achieve eternal Life.

The second, or instant, contains tranquility in the subtle body, which is spread throughout the body by the Spinal Cord.

By means of the subtle elements, it can be felt throughout the body by the external senses which are made of the five elements. This inner Tranquility, however, cannot be perceived by the onlooker.

With the practice of twelve Kriyas, or Pranayams of Tranquil Air, one interiorization, or one Pratyahara, is held.

By the practice of 144 Kriyas of Tranquil Air, true Dharana, or Tranquility, is formed.

By the practice of 1,728 Pranayams, the true state of Dhyana, or meditation, is held, and by the practice of Pranayam 20,736 times, Oneness-Attunement between the seeking individual self and the pure, supreme Self is held.

When the seeker achieves the state of Oneness between these two aspects of the ultimate Self and remains attuned at that state spontaneously, it is called Yoga. This is naturally held at the After-effect-poise of Kriya

Kriyar Parabastha

If the Yogi practices such a state of Oneness twelve times, then he overcomes the influence of time, and eventually the influence of death, and thereby, he attains the everlasting Life.

The whole practice of higher Kriyas and achieving that state is a matter of sincere practice of Kriya in a righteous way under the direct and personal instruction of Gurudev, or the Master.

**Aghosambyanjanamaswarancha,
akanthatalosthamanasikancha.
Arephajat mubhayosthabarjitang, jadaksharang na kharate kadachit.**

Aghosha is that which does not make sound; *Abyanjana* is that which is not seen; *Aswara* is that which if remembered does not make sound. It is not possible to utter them by the throat, palate, or lips. Neither it is possible to utter or make their sounds by the nose or palate. The Self, the body of eternal Omkar, has no lips. Beyond it there is Kutastha (which can only be known through the words of the Guru, personally received).

The sound of *OM* is beyond the senses; it is inner sound. Beyond this inner sound is Kutastha, the inner Self. Lahiri Mahasay using atypical Bengali or Sanskrit phrase advises,

Guru-bakya-gamya

meaning that it can only be realized through the words of the Guru. It is clear by this statement that the disciple must learn it personally from his Guru, or Master.

**Jenaso pasyate margang, Pranasten hi gachhyati.
Ata samavyasennityang sanmargagamanaya bai.**

Whoever sees this path (by the help of his Guru) finds his life force transcended. That is, at the After-effect-poise of Kriya, the life force is dissolved in Brahma, the ultimate Self, Tranquility. For this reason, the seeker should practice day and night just to have the path.

When the seeker sees the path by the practice of Yonimudra in between the eyebrows (which can be known personally from the Guru), his life force dissolves into Tranquility at the After-effect-poise of Kriya.

The seeker should always sincerely practice Kriyas to find this path of inner Realization in the inner Light between the eyebrows.

Hrid dwarang bayudwarancha, urdhadwaramata param.
Moksha dwara bilanchaiba, susirang mandalang bidu.

Heart is the Life Force from the dorsal center to between the eyebrows. Tranquilizing that state of breath between the eyebrows in Kutastha, a Star is seen. When that Star bursts, a door reveals.

The opening of the door after the Star is door of the heart.

This also is the door of air which is felt at the After-effect-poise of Kriya (Kriyar Parabastha).

The door above is understood only by the practitioners of Kriya upon feeling the head to be heavy.

The seeker's entry into the atom of Brahma, the ultimate Self, is the door to Liberation. At that time, the mind does not go outwardly to attachments and worldly bondage.

The whole world exists in one part of that atom.

Then the seeker sees the inner beatific Visions, or Revelations, and eventually he dissolves himself in the very atom of the Self.

The place of dissolution is in between the eyebrows.

There one is no more. and one has nothing anymore. Therefore. Liberation is felt a bit there at the After-effect-poise of Kriya.

Susirang: the seeker's remaining attuned at the inner beatific State of Consciousness beyond these qualities.

Mandalang: the seeker's experience of

Sarbang Brahmamagang iagat

"the world is Brahma, the ultimate Self."

When the seeker tranquilizes the breath between the eyebrows inhaling through the Spinal Cord, he sees. Kutastha, the inner Self.

Then Kutastha Bindu, the dazzling Star of Consciousness, is seen between the eyebrows by the practice of Yonimudra.

When the Star of Consciousness bursts, then the seeker finds the door of the heart, the core of Consciousness (not the muscular organ).

For the Yogi, the heart is in between the eyebrows.

The door of the heart is also the door of Tranquil Air. Only this Tranquil Air in the poised state takes the seeker into the door above into the head of one thousand petals.

Then the seeker can enter into the subtle atom of Brahma, the ultimate Self. When the seeker enters into the atom of Brahma, the ultimate Self, then he finds the inner door of Liberation between the eyebrows.

In fact, Illumination starts at the heart, between the eyebrows, then goes to the head, then back to the heart (between the eyebrows) and Liberation is attained.

This door of Tranquil Air is the door to inner Realization. The seeker's mind is then so inwardly confirmed that it does not look outwardly to worldly things, i.e., bondage, or attachment.

The whole world, in fact, exists in one part of the atom of Brahma, the ultimate Self.

This is a state of subtle dualism. The seeker is a seer, and he sees the inner beatific mysterious Revelations and Visions. When he dissolves himself in that atom of pure Consciousness, he loses the character of the seer and merges into Oneness with the ultimate Self which is felt at the After-effect-poise of Kriya.

Then he is on the absolute ground of the Spontaneous, the natural state of pure Consciousness, beyond the three qualities:

1. Tamasik (negative),

2. Rajasik (positive), and

3. Sattvik (divine).

At this stage, the seeker is in eternal Oneness with the ultimate Self, and is, therefore, beyond all thoughts and intellect. He is one with the ultimate Self as well as one with the universe.

**Bhayang krodhamalasyamati swapnatijagaram.
Atyaharamanaharang nityang Yogi bibarjayet.**

There are certain things to renounce. For example, the fear of seeing something. Consider yourself to be little and treat others as big; therefore, the little one cannot be angry with the big ones.

In anger, one loses the hold of the Self, and the mind moves from Brahma and falls into hell.

The seeker should not practice Kriya in a lethargic way but with full attention, immediately, without delay. Only then can good work be done.

In long sleep, the life force is affected; therefore, the body is hampered. Staying awake at night increases tension. Due to absence of *Bramhagni*, inner Energy, diseases are likely to attack. Overeating generates suffering in one as everybody can understand. In fasting when one does not eat at all, how can the life force, which is generated from food, continue? So eat as much as you feel to sustain the body. One should always pay attention to all of these.

The verse deals with the practical aspects of a yogi 's life, pointing to a balanced way of life.

The yogi should not be idle but remain alert and sincere in his practice of Kriya. He should not indulge in overeating. Nor should he fast, but rather he should eat in a balanced way to generate life force in the body. The yogi does not eat for sense enjoyment but to sustain the body for the practice of Kriya.

He should treat himself as nothing to destroy egoism, pride and anger. Anger is the great enemy of realizing the ultimate Self. It destroys inward attention for inner Realization and puts the seeker on a negative track.

**Anena bidhina samang, nityamvyasyata kramat.
Swayam mupadyate jnanang, trivirmasairna sangsaya.**

But if one practices everyday according to the instructions for three continuous months, the knowledge will be automatically produced.

If the seeker practices Kriya according to the advice laid down above, strictly according to the instructions he receives from his Guru continuously for three months with utmost sincerity, then inner Realization will be automatically revealed, and he will attain the Knowledge of the Self.

Chaturvi pasyate Devan, panchavistulyabikrama.
Ichhayapnoti Kaibalyang, sasthemasi na sangsaya.

Within four months of sincere Kriya practice, the seeker will see the gods. Within five months, he will become powerful like them.

Bikrama: Gradually and naturally, he will become like the gods having mysterious powers.

Kaibyalyang: Attaining the state of eternal Tranquility by the practice of Kebali Kumbhaka is Kaibalya. The mind becomes pure, freed from attachment, and the tranquil subtle Air of breathing is alerted like a straight-standing stick from the coccygeal center. This Breath is the tranquil Kundalini up to between. the eyebrows. It remains alerted and can be likened to the holding of the reins of running horses.

By practicing Kriya for four months according to advice, the seeker can see the gods; by five months, he can acquire mysterious powers like the gods.

Eventually, by sincere Kriya practice, he attains the Tranquil Breath and thereby automatically and naturally attains Peace in that poised state of Breath.

The mind is purified from attachments, and the intellect is poised in inner Wisdom.

The life force is felt as though it were a stick standing straight reaching up from the coccygeal center to between the eyebrows. Kundalini, the mysterious Energy, becomes tranquil. The person feels alerted from the coccygeal center to the medulla oblongata as though lightly holding the rems of running horses.

**Parthiba panchamatrani, chaturmatrani varuno.
Agneyastu trimatrani, dwimatra marutastatha.**

Parthibi (earth): The world evolves from five subtle states, *Pancho-tanmatra*.

One percent of water is there in the soil of the earth; one percent of fire is there; one percent of air is there; one percent of ether or *Akasa* is there; and four percent of earth is there.

This physical body is produced from earth by the father's semen. That semen is made from the earth from the eating of food. It consists of the following five subtle states:

1. four percent earth (meat, bones, hair, nails, etc.),

2. one-fourth part water (blood), and

3. the rest is fire,

4. air and

5. ether (or void).

Varuna (water): having four *matra* (durations of rhythms of vibrations of consciousness):

1. one above [head],

2. one of the tongue [soft palate],

3. mucous of the nose,

4. mucous of the eyes,

5. ear wax,

6. below [the logs],

7. the navel,

8. penis.

9. rectum, and

10. pores.

Between the above and the below is water.
Three nerves:

1. Ida,

2. Pingala, and

3. Susumna [the Spinal Cord].

Inside the Spine there is water, i.e., Saraswati [Divine Mother, the Goddess of Knowledge, music, and rhythms] in Brahmanari, the nerve of Brahma.

That water is Karanbari, or "causal water."

He is the Cause of all causes as the individual pervading throughout the world.

No place exists where Jivas, or individuals, are not. Jivas are the manifestation of Siva. In other words, the individual being becomes Lord Siva, the all-pervading ultimate Self, or Brahma [in the state of inner Realization].

Agni (the fire): There are three types of fire, which contains three matras:

1. Ordinary fire,

2. The fire in the navel which moves the physical body, and

3. Brahmagni, the fire of the ultimate Self, produced when the same fire of the navel is tranquil. That fire is not like ordinary fire. The sun and the radiation of the moon are not there. It is such a state which reveals all, yet there is no light. It is the state of inner Realization.

Bayu, or *Maruta* (air): There are two types of air [Breath], which contains two matras:

1. Restless air, and

2. Tranquil Air.

The restless air is in the breathing of all individuals, and the tranquil Air at the After-effect-poise of Kriya is in the Yogi.

This verse and the next one deal with the science of *manifestation*. There are five states of vibration which come into the awareness to the seeker. They are comprehended differently as state of elements:

1. the solid state of vibration, or the earth element,

2. the liquid state of vibration, or the water element,

3. the subgaseous state of vibration, or the fire element,

4. the gaseous state of vibration, or the air element, and

5. the ethereal state of vibration, or the ether element.

All the other states of vibrations are in the earth element condensed in some subtle form and percentage called "Pancha-tanmatra", or the five subtle states.

The physical body represents the earth element and is produced from the semen of the father, which is produced from earth element from foodstuff. So the physical body contains the entire universe in the condensed form. The short description is stated here.

In the body, the water element is present in the above, i.e., in the head, tongue, nose, eyes and ears, and it is present below, i.e., at the navel, penis, rectum and pores. The water element is also present in the nerves of Ida, Pingala and Susumna (Spinal Cord). It is even in the subtle nerve inside the Spinal Cord called *Brahmanari*. Water is called Karanbari, the Cause of all causes, the basis of all individuals of the universe. When individuals are everywhere in manifestation, the seeker is freed from manifestation. Then the same individual becomes supreme Being. Again, fire is present in the body at the navel, and this fire moves the body and digests food. When this fire, or energy, is tranquilized by the practice of Pranayam, or Kriya including *Omkar Kriyas* and *Navi (navel) Kriya*, then Agni, the same energy, or fire, becomes *Brahmagni*, mystic Energy, which is different than ordinary fire, or energy.

This Brahmagni, or mystic Energy, reveals all the beatific inner visions, or Revelations, which are free from the sun, moon and fire. That is, the sun, moon and fire are unable to reveal such.

There is no light there, yet due to mystic Energy everything is revealed there. This is the state of inner Revelations.

Air (Maruta, or Bayu) is present in the physical body as breathing. This air is of two kinds:

1. Chanchal Bayu (restless air), which is present in all individual beings, and

2. Sthira Bayu (Tranquil Air, or Breath).

In fact, this restless air is the cause of this entire manifestation and movements.

When this restless air of breathing is tranquilized by the practice of scientific Kriyas, or Pranayams, including Omkar Kriyas, then it becomes Tranquil Air.

This Tranquil Air is present in the Yogi at the After-effect-poise of Kriya

Kriyar Parabastha

When the Tranquil Air is attained by the practice of Pranayam, or scientific Kriyas, then the Yogi is free from manifestation.

The restless air of breathing is the real cause of the awareness of this entire manifestation. So when the restless air of the breathing is tranquilized, immediately the manifestation of this entire universe vanishes, being unreal. At that state the Yogi is beyond space and time.

He is in such a marvelous state of Consciousness at the After-effect-poise of Kriya that he acts and yet he does not act, he speaks yet he is silent, simply because everything has become One Consciousness and he has no attachment towards the results of his actions.

The scripture describes his state as *Jivanmukta*, "one who is liberated while living in the physical body."

**Ekamatrastathakaso, ardhamatrancha chintayet.
Siddhing krittva tu manasa, chintayedatmanatmani.**

Akasa: "ether." Ether is the subtle state of one medium for the inner form of revelation.

ardhamatra: "1/2 accent." The 1/2 accent is a part of the form of One. That is, the whole world exists in one part of that atom of Brahma, the ultimate Self. This is a state where there is no sound, no individual self and no purpose. Nor is it possible to understand one's thoughts. It is an amazing state, and there the mind is dissolved.

The restless air of breath is called "mind." When the same restless air of breathing becomes Tranquil, then the mind is merged, or dissolved. It is the mind which moves and wanders in all directions, but when it is tranquilized, its movement stops.

When the mind is merged, then there is no desire anymore. When there is no desire for anything, then one gets all things without having anything.

Therefore, the Self finds the spontaneous states, that is, the After-effect-poise of Kriya, in its own course.

This verse continues to deal with the science of manifestation. The earth, water, fire and air elements are respectively connected with the coccygeal, sacral, lumbar and dorsal centers in the Spinal Cord. Ether is connected with the cervical center, which is the subtle medium of awareness.

When the seeker of Truth raises receiving capacities to it higher vibrational level by dissolving the lower state of vibration in the lower centers, than he is in this subtle state of vibration.

Ether is the medium of receiving the ethereal state of Consciousness. Beyond this state, there is a rhythm of half-accent sound which acts between the cervical center and the eyebrows.

At this state in one part of the atom of Brahma, the whole world rests. Here there is no sound, no individual and no purpose; yet there is intelligence beyond comprehension. This is an amazing state of Awareness.

The restless air of breathing is called mind. When the seeker, by the sincere practice of Kriya, tranquilizes the restless air of breathing in between the eyebrows, the mind is dissolved and the intellect is poised in the inner Wisdom of eternal Realization.

All desires are transcended, and there is no more craving of the mind for outward things. Then the individual attains all, that is, fuller life, without having anything. This is called highest Happiness and highest Attainment.

At the After-effect-poise of Kriya, the seeker attains eternal Tranquility, or Peace, through this Tranquil Breath.

In summary, restless breath is the cause of the manifested world. When the seeker tranquilizes restless breath through the scientific practice of Pranayam, the whole manifestation is tranquil, the world of thoughts and intellect of the individual is silenced, and the seeker is poised in inner Wisdom.

The breath has an inseparable relationship with thoughts and sounds. So by tranquilizing breathing and transcending sound, the seeker can transcend thoughts and silence the intellect, making it poised.

This describes the science of manifestation and how to achieve eternal Tranquility beyond manifestation.

Tringsat parbangula Prano, jatra Prana pratistha.
Esa Prana iti khyato, bajya Prana sagochara.

From the coccygeal center upto Brahmarandhra, the aperture of Brahma at the head, is thirty fingers, where Prana, the life force, remains attuned as told before. This is called Prana, the life force. Bajya Prana, the life force of outside, can be seen.

The tranquilizing of breath by the practice of Kriya and the tranquilizing of life force from the coccygeal to the aperture of Brahma in the head is called "the true state of Prana."

The breath of the outside in manifestation, which is restless, is the external life force.

To realize the eternal Being or eternal Nectar (Amrita), in other words, the eternal Tranquility, the seeker must attain the Tranquil Air inside the Spinal Cord which is true Prana, the life force.

Asitisatasatachaiba sahasrani trayodasa.
Lakshaschasikoapi niswasa ahoratra pramanato.

When breathing is faster, then in one day and one night respiration can flow up to 113,680 times. Normally during the same time, the figure is 21,600 times.

During a day and night, if respiration is faster than usual, the breath can flow in and out 113,680 times. Normally, in the course of a day and night, there are 21,600 breaths.

This figure is reduced by Kriya practice to 2,000 times. So, breathing 1,000 times in the day and 1,000 times in the night, in a normal course, provides greater Tranquility to a Yogi.

One of his breaths takes about 44 seconds.

Such a Yogi is matured in Kriya practice.

Thoughts are inseparably related to breathing. So, when the number of breaths is reduced, proportionately thoughts are reduced.

Eventually, with the tranquilization of breath, thoughts are dissolved. Thereby, the seeker can attain the After-effect-poise of Kriya, or eternal Tranquility, which is *Amrita, nectar proper.*

Prana adyo Hridi sthane, Apanastu punargude.
Samano navidese tu, Udana kanthamasrita.

**Byana sarbesu changesu sada babritya tisthati.
Atha varnastu panchanag Pranadinamanukramat.**

Prana, the life forces that operate in the physical body are as follows:

Prana operates in front of the body from the heart; Apana operates at the coccygeal center; Samana operates at the navel center (Navi); Udana operates at the throat (Kantha); and Byana operates throughout the body. This is the description of five Pranas.

In fact, there is just one Prana, the life force, which takes different names while operating in different parts of the body. Out of these forty-nine types, there are five primary Pranas. They are as follows:

1. Prana (appropriation),

2. Apana (rejection, or elimination),

3. Samana (assimilation),

4. Udana (regeneration), and

5. Byana (distribution).

They operate respectively at the heart, coccyx, navel, throat and throughout the body.

The practice of scientific Kriyas, namely, Pranayams, or Kriyas, is entrusted to tranquilize Prana and Apana, while the practice of Mahamudra is entrusted to tranquilize Upana and Byana, and the practice of Navi Kriya is entrusted to tranquilize Samana.

Thus, on the one hand, Kriyas, including Omkar Kriyas and the practice of Mahamudra and Navi Kriya, help to tranquilize the five different states of Prana into one tranquil state.

On the other hand, the practice of *Khecharimudra*, or *Talabya Kriya*, transcends the attachment towards smell, taste and liquids.

The practice of Yonimudra, or Beatific Inner Revelations Kriya, transcends attachment towards physical beauty or form, i.e., vision or light and sound.

When these two Mudras are practiced in an integrated way, then the operation of withdrawing from all the five senses of attachment is scientifically accomplished.

Mahamuni Babaji taught Yogiraj Sri Sri Shyama Charan Lahiri Mahasay the practice of Yonimudra and Khecharimudra, or Talabya Kriya, in an integrated way, combining the two, which simultaneously withdraw the focus of attention, or attachment, from the five senses (tasting, smelling, touching, seeing and hearing). This forms the traditional of original Kriya.

Any amendment to the teachings of original Kriya, especially to the point of integrations of Yonimudra and Kecharimudra, creates a loophole in scientifically and simultaneously withdrawing the five sense organs. This results in failure to achieve Pratyahar, or interioization, and a higher state of Consciousness. Without being established in Khechari, or Talabya Kriya, the seeker is not introduced to Omkar Kriyas, which in original Kriya tradition are Kriyas of the Tranquil Breath, or Sthira Bayu.

**Raktavarna maniprakhya Pranobayo prakirtita.
Apanastasya madhye tu Indragopaka sanniva.**

In Prana the diamond is seen like the color of blood.

While in the atom of Apana, there are five states of vibration like indragops (the name of a certain insect) that are white, black and mixed in color.

When the seeker practices Yonimudra with Tranquil Breath, he sees a dazzling sun of Consciousness between the eyebrows. When in the lower centers in the atom of the life force; the five states of vibration seem to be black and white in color.

**Samanastasya madhye tu, gokshira sphatika prava.
Apandur Udanastu, Byanoyapyarchisama prava.**

The color of Samana Bayu is like white milk or marble stone. Udana has a white and yellow color. Byana has a color throughout the body like a burning flame.

The verse continues to deal with the color of the different types of life force.

By the practice of Navi Kriya at the navel, the seeker can see the white energy in operation in tranquilizing Samana Bayu. The practice of Mahamudra tranquilizes the white and yellow-color of Udana Bayu at the throat. Byana Bayu throughout the whole physical .body is like the color of a burning flame tranquilized by the practice of Mahamudra..

Jasaisa mandalang vittva, maruto jati murdhani.
Jatra tatra mriyedwapi, na sa bhuyoyavijayate.

When all these centers are passed through and Prana, the life force, enters the head, then if the seekers body drops off here and there, having been, he has not been, that is, he is tuned automatically into the atom of Brahma the ultimate Self, forever. It is a mysterious state.

When the seeker attains the perfect Tranquil Air by the practice of Pranayam and passes through all the centers inside the Spinal Cord, then he attains the Tranquil Air at the head.

When he is tuned in Oneness with the supreme Being, then wherever or whenever his physical body drops off does not matter, as he is in Oneness with the supreme Being. So he is in the eternal Being.

Chapter 3

The Niralamba
Upanisad

Without Substratum, Having no *Abalamban*, Support

Ni - Without, *abalamba* - support or substratum

Om. What is Brahma?

Brahma [the ultimate Self] is beyond all signs or titles, without beginning or end, pure, tranquil, beyond qualities, without substratum, eternally blissful, infinite, blissful nectar, absolute without a second, and consciousness.

What is Sabala Brahma?

Sa means "to go", *bala* means "being in the inexplicable state at the After-effect-poise of Kriya"; the great cosmic ego on the universal plane which apparently is a great sheath wrapped up with ignorance of the five elements, earth, water, fire, air and ether, and is floating in all kinds of reasonings.

What is Iswara Brahma?

It is that Brahma, the ultimate Self, who has adhered to the energy of Prakriti, Nature, entered into the lokas, or spheres, and after having duly created them, and become the acting agent of regulating principle of the desires. [This is the state of Iswara .]

What is Jiva Brahma?

Brahma and Visnu are the form of names. I am in the gross form of knowledge when I identify myself with the body parts.

What is Prakriti Brahma?

It is the energy of Brahma in the form of intelligence from the ethereal sky [ethereal or cosmic dimensions]. It has the various forms of abilities to create the state of manifestation.

What is Paramatma Brahma?

Beyond the body is Brahma, the supreme Self (Kutastha).

What is Brahmadi Brahma?

That Brahma, the ultimate Self, is Brahma, the Creator, Siva, Akshara (eternity), Indra (king of gods), Visnu, Lord of preservation of the manifestation, Rudra (the lord of energy), Sage Manu (the father of mankind), Surya (the Sun), Chandra (the Moon), Sura (the devatas, gods) and pisacha (ungods); and He is all.

What is Jati Brahnma?

The self has no caste; the caste, or jati, is imagined in application of the term.

What is Karma Brahma?

Karma is defined as the state of Sthirattva in Atma, the Self.

What is Akarma?

It is attachment to egoism and doership, that which has resulted from the birth, and performing all Karmas, actions, with the expectation of results therefrom. In other words, all actions are Akarmas, inactions, if performed with expectation of results.

What is Tapa Brahma?

Tapa Brahma is knowledge of Kutastha.
That is, Brahma, the ultimate Self is alone true and real, and jagat, the world, is false, or unreal.

What is Asura Brahma?

Tapa (meditation) with pride, is Asura Brahma.

What is Jnana Brahma?

It is restraining the senses to worship Guru through sravan (hearing), manan (analyzing), nididdhasana (surrendering to Lord), seeing Brahma, the ultimate Self, in all and realization of the Self.

What is Ajnana Brahma?

The knowledge of husband and wife, the knowledge of the stations of life [the four divisions of Vedic lifestyle : brahmacharchya (student lifestyle), grihastha (householder lifestyle), vanaprastha (lifestyle of the forest recluse), and sanyas (renunciate lifestyle)], the knowledge of bondage and liberation are but the knowledge of imagination.

What is Sangsara Brahma?

Unending ignorance, desires, birth, and death, are sixfold illusion [the world].

What is Bandha Brahma?

Bondage is to live in household lifestyle with attachment, to perform rituals and vows, and to make gifts with expectation of results.

What is Moksha Brahma?

Moksha, or liberation, is to be free of desires.

What is Sukha Brahma?

Sukha, or Happiness, is the state of After-effect-poise of Kriya.

What is Dukha Brahma?

Dukha, or suffering, is not to hold onto the Self.

What is Swarga Brahma?

Swarga, or heaven, is to hold onto the true Self.

What is Naraka Brahma?

Naraka, or hell, is to hold onto the not-self.

What is Parama pada Brahma?

Oneness with Brhma, the ultimate Self.

What is Upasya?

Upasya, or the object of meditation, is to hold onto the Consciousness of Guru, the Self, throughout the body within. That Guru, or Atma (the Self) is He upon whom one is required to meditate.

What is Bidwan Brahma?

Bidwan, or wise, is he who knows the true supreme Self in all beings.

What is murha Brahma?

Murha, or ignorant, is he who possesses the sense of egoism, doership and treats himself as the enjoyer.

What is Sanyasi Brahma?

Sanyasi (Swami), or renunciate, is he who holds onto the ultimate Self while renouncing every kind of result of his actions.

What is grajya?

Grajya, or objects to which are worth paying attention, is that which brings benefits [righteousness].

What is agrajya Brahma?

Agrajya, or objects to which are not worth paying attention, is to be outward; it is the paying of attention by the mind to things other than Atma, the Self.

What is Samadhi?

Samadhi is to be in Oneness with the ultimate Self upon having been freed from attachment and egoism.

Chapter 4

The Taitiriya Upanisad : On Education

The oriental lifestyle of the Hindu people is guided and regulated strictly in accordance with their holy scripture, the Veda (the book of absolute Knowledge, or inner Wisdom), and so their culture is known as "Vedic culture."

Vedic culture divides the span of a man's life into four periods:

1. Brahmacharya Asram, student life,

2. Grihastha Asram, householder life,

3. Vanaprastha, retired life in the forest in seclusion, and

4. Sanyas, renunciate life.

Each period covers twenty-five years, projecting a lifespan of one hundred years.

Brahmacharya Asram

Traditionally, when young boys donned the sacred thread at the age of eight, they were sent away by their parents to reside at the Master's home, or hermitage. Here they would remain for seventeen years to study various teachers. In order to build strong character and a foundation for righteous lifestyle, the boys could not visit their parents during this period, nor could their parents visit them. The Master would assume total financial responsibility for the food and shelter of the students, and the students would meditate and study while learning such practicalities as gardening, dairy work, etc, according to the Master's guidance.

At the end of the seventeen years, a convocation (Samavarta) would be held by the Master, who would question the student on what he had learned during his long residence at the hermitage.

A story from the Upanisads can be cited here about one such Samavarta:

A certain Master turned to his students who were about to leave the hermitage. "What is meant by *Da* ?" he questioned.

One student who had developed the Bramanic, or sattvik spirit, from his education replied, "Da means Damana [literally, 'to master', ' to overcome'], that is, to dissolve the senses."

Another student who had developed the khatriya, or rajasik, spirit from his education replied, "Da means Dana ['to give," 'to donate'], that is, to donate or give to others without having expectations for profit and return.

A third student who had developed a tamasika spirit answered, "Da means Damana ['to put down'], that is, to supress others with force.

So the first student and the third student answered with the same word, Damana, but how they interpreted this word was entirely different. The Master remained silent, but he knew what each student had learned.

The Brahmacharya education in the Master's house for seventeen years and the Samavarta convocation provided the student with an inner education that served as a foundation for the rest of his life starting with householder lifestyle.

So the spirit of Brahmacharya Asram is man-making and character-building.

Grihastha Asram Thereafter, the student returned to his parents who, with much consideration, arranged his marriage.

He then assumed the responsibilities of a householder for the next twenty- five years.

The Grihastah Asram, or householder lifestyle, had the responsibility of providing for the other three lifestyles in terms of food and support. Soon the newly established householder would become a young father.

Vanaprastha Asram The grandfather who now saw his grandson and ascertained that his lineage would continue, retired to the forest with his wife to lead a spiritual life for the third twenty-five year span of life.

Sanyas Asram Finally, at the age of seventy-five, the man would enter into renunciate life to complete the fourth twenty-five years.

These are the four stages of life style in Vedic culture. When the sons are sent away by their parents to live at the Master' s hermitage, an important ceremony of Vedic lifestyle called Upanayana Sanskara is held. During this ceremony, sacred threads are placed on the boy to protect him from outwardness, and he receives instruction from a Brahmana, priest, Yogi, or Swami on how to practice Pranayam according to the Vedic lifestyle through a particular Mantra (syllable), called *Gayatri Mantra*.

Gayatri is the Divine Mother of absolute Knowledge, the Energy of the ultimate Self, which is awakened through the practice of Pranayam, inhaling and exhaling that involves the seven centers of the spine which are as follows:

1. Coccygeal center, the earth element (Bhu),

2. Sacral center, the water element (Bhuba),

3. Lumbar center, the fire element (Swa),

4. Dorsal center, the air element (Maha),

5. Cervical center, the ether element (Jana),

6. Medulla oblongata or the center between the eye-brows, where resides the atom of the inner Self, Kutastha (Tapa), and

7. Thousand petals at the head where vibrate the rhythms of Truth (Satya).

Bhu, Bhuba, Swa, Maha, Jana, Tapa and Satya are the lokas, or spheres, of particular states of vibration of different dimensions of pure Consciousness of the ultimate Self.

The Gayatri Mantra involves chanting in the right places to receive the vibrations of inner Light and inner Sound through which the student will attain higher Consciousness.

Sage Taitiriya clearly explains the spirit of Vedic education in his treatise called Taitiriya Upanisad.

In the hermitage of the Guru (Gurugriha), the students truly learn how to properly chant Vedic hymns and to master the vibrations and rhythms behind the letters (A, Aa, E, Ei, like A, B, & C) which represent the inner Light and inner Sound as well as OM (AUM), Amen, Amin.

The Master teaches them proper chanting, Sanskrit grammar, and the practice of Pranayam based on Breath with Gayatri Mantra:

Om Bhur Bhuba Swa Tat Sabitur barenag bhargo devasya dhimahi. dhiyo yona prochodayat

Master and students together are dedicated to this spirit of inner education which lays the foundation for achieving the egoless state of Consciousness through meditation.

From the viewpoint of realization, however, the four divisions of life have a deeper, more significant meaning which the reader will learn as this book unfolds.

The Taitiriya Upanisad will spell out the true system of education, the righteous way to realize Truth, the ultimate Self.

4.1 First Advice

Mitra means "Sun." Varuna* means "that which is seen in Kutastha (the inner Self in between the eyebrows)"; it resembles water.

Kutastha is the Sun where the supreme Person resides resting upon Varuna, the waters [the rhythm of Consciousness].

He is Kutastha, the divine Eye. His image is the Eye of Brahma. He is Guru of all, and He is Vrihaspati [Vrihat, "big"; Pati, "Lord"].

Steadfast Tranquility in Brahma [the ultimate Self] is called Visnu [the state of Tranquility]. To stay in that state of Tranquility is Eternity. This Eternity is Bliss.

Varuna itself which means "water" or "the god of water" refers to the rhythms of vibrations of consciousness which are seen by the practice of Yonimudra in between the eyebrows.

In the practice of Yonimudra colors are seen in between the eyebrows. The dazzling bright yellow color which appears can be likened to fire, or the sun. Around it appears a bluish color which is the supreme Person. Actually, it only appears blue to the ordinary eyes because of the high voltage of its energy. Also are patches of color which appear like waves on the lake are rhythms of consciousness.

When the seeker by the practice of Omkar Kriyas (the Kriyas of the tranquil Breath, higher Kriyas of meditation) followed by the practice of Yonimudra, sees the radiant inner Self in between the eyebrows and attains Tranquility, he attains Eternity and Bliss.

What can be said above about the supreme, pure Being is that He is Bliss and is attained by Kriyas of the [Tranquil] Air. That Air is Brahma and Eternity.

The Tranquil Breath is Eternity. When the Omkar Kriyas are practiced on the background of the Tranquil Breath with the help of Talabya Kriya, the Kriyanwita seeker attains the state of eternal Tranquility, or eternal Bliss.

Whatever is said is true.

This is because the creation, or birth, takes place by entering into the atom of Brahma by the air of Brahma through His perfectly desireless desire.

By the perfectly desireless desire of the ultimate Self, the Tranquil Breath becomes restless. In other words, creation, or manifestation, starts.

There is no fault in saying many times: "Thou art Brahma! Please protect me! Protect the utterer! All are Brahma."

All melt into Oneness at the After-effect-poise of Kriya ,which is the transcendental state.

OM! Santi! Santi! Santi!

All negative vibrations become peaceful Brahma. To make it emphatically clear, Santi is repeated three times.

First, the seeker must tranquilize the vibrations into Peace.

Then, he must practice Kriya to attain the Tranquil Breath that will lead him to eternal Tranquility, or Peace. To attain Tranquility is the aim of everybody's life.

4.2   Second Advice

It is necessary to know the proper way of education in order to attain Knowledge.

The essence of education lies in the proper chanting of the hymns of the scriptures.

To receive true education for inner Realization of the ultimate Self, the seeker must learn the proper way to utter or chant the hymns of the Vedas.

In other words, in order to educate himself for the attainment of the pure Vibration of Sabda, or "inner Sound,

" to attain inner Realization, the seeker must learn how to properly chant the Mantras (composed of letters and words).

The sanskrit word Varna means vowels, like A, E, I, 0 and U.

While the Sanskrit word Sabda means "sound," and it also means "word."

So by "Words of God" is meant "inner Sound." Sound of vibrations are of three kinds:

1. Udattva (loud),

2. . Anudattva (slow), and

3. Swarita (gentle).

Matra, or signs, are of three kinds:

1. Hraswa (short),

2. Dirgha (long), and

3. Pluto (lingering).

The strength of Prana, or life force, is of two kinds:

1. Swalpa Prana (small life force), and

2. Mahaprana (great life force).

In the vowels and consonants listing] the odd number letters, 1, 3, and 5 contain the small life force [energy] and the even letters, 2 and 4, contain the great life force [energy].

The Sama Veda , the means of proper chanting, contains in detail the vibrations and rhythms of hymns and their chanting. There are seven kinds of tuning:

1. Saraja (Sa),

2. Risava(Re),

3. Gandhar (Ga),

4. Madhyam (Ma),

5. Pancham (Pa),

6. Dhaibat (Dha), and

7. Nikhada (Ni).

There are three degrees of pitches:

1. Udara (low),

2. Mudara/Madhyama medium), and

3. Tara (high).

So we have seven times three which all together make up twenty-one types of rhythms.

The seven types of Swara [notes, or tunings] arising from Navi [the navel], is called Udara [low].

The seven types Swara [notes, or tunings] rising higher than this is called Mudara (Madhyama) [medium].

The extremely high pitches of the seven Swara [notes, or tunings] are Called Tara [high].

They are all Sons, the means of chanting of Sama Veda, the Veda of chantings. All these are component parts of inner education for attaining Knowledge.

The following five points are the vedangas, or "the subsidiaries to the Vedas."

1. Siksha (Education),

2. Varna (Letters),

3. Swara (Notes, or Tuning),

4. Matra (top Signs), and

5. Bala (Strength).

There are five sons, or means of education, in the Sama Veda.

The inner Realization of the ultimate Self is possible only

through proper inner education.

Education involves mastering the rhythms and vibrations of inner Light and inner Sound by the practice of Kriyas, or Pranayams, and help of the aforementioned five subsidiary means.

Spiritually speaking, the essence of education lies in learning the proper way of chanting the hymns which involve generating vibrations of pure Energy beyond concept, thought, intellect and ego.

The Energy of the life force is found in two different degrees:

1. Small, and

2. Great.

According to the rhythms of tunings and the chanting of the letters these two degrees of energy are found in the atom of inner Light and inner Sound.

The letters are, in fact, not mere letters. They represent the proper inner Light (Jyoti) and inner Sound (Swara) of the strength of Energy (Bala).

So in mastering the proper chanting of letters or Varna (inner Sound), one can learn and grow to the true path of attaining inner Knowledge or Wisdom of the ultimate Self through the sound of OM.

The small degree of energy is associated with the letter numbers 1, 3 and 5 of each Barga, or "line of the alphabet, " while the greater degree of energy is connected with the letter numbers 2 and 4 of each Barga, or "line of the alphabet. "

Thus, Mantra is directly associated with inner Sound, and chanting, or Japam, leads to inner Realization through inner Sound, or OM.

Thus, education is not a matter of mere literacy, the ability to read and write. Rather education means to regulate and conduct daily life in a righteous manner in order that the seeker attains the inner Realization of the ultimate Self.

By mastering the proper vibrations of the letters, inner Sound, going Eeyond thoughts, concepts, meanings and intellect, the seeker dissolves into t e new dimension of inner Light and inner Sound, and eventually into the inner Realization of the ultimate Self or Lord : the ultimate Existence, Consciousness and Bliss.

4.3 Third Advice

What I relate to you is in accordance with the advice of the Guru, the Master.

If I were to tell an untruth, then it would reflect badly on the reputation of the Master. In other words, the Guru would be teaching an untruth.

By relating Truth, both Master and disciple are glorified in Truth.

Do you know what *Brahma barchasa* is?

When holding onto the ultimate Self, Brahma, Energy is generated in the Guru and disciple. Know that it is Brahma barchasa.

If I were to speak an untruth, then our [Guru and disciple] study of the Veda would be imperfect. If our study of the Veda is to be perfect and complete, listen to whatever I say.

The Guru and disciple meditate or practice together to generate Energy in order to attain Oneness with the ultimate Self Brahma.

If the study or practice is completed, or, in other words, if by the Kriya practice the intellect is dissolved, the state of Tranquility, or inner Wisdom, is attained.

After explaining Karma Kanda, or "the nature of actions," I will explain the Taitiriya Upanisad, which contains the Knowledge the ultimate Self, or Brahma.

Upanisad can be broken down into *Upa* meaning "near" and *nisad* meaning "whatever is uttered beyond a doubt by Guru, or the Master."

The disciples learn them accordingly by the practice of Kriya.

Advice on Para Vidya, or "transcendental Knowledge" and apara Vidya, or "imminent Knowledge" is given in the Tantra and the Veda.

The state beyond the end when the intellect dissolves in the stage of culmination, is Brahma, the ultimate Self.

To be Tranquil in that ultimate Self is called Upanisad. Later, whatever I explain is Upanisad.

The dissolving of the intellect by the seeker through Kriya practice under the direct guidance of his Guru, or Master, and attainment of Oneness with the ultimate Self (Brahma) is the state of eternal Tranquility. This state is called "Upanisad. "

In the five states of Brahma, there are five places. I will explain whatever one realizes if one stays in those five states.

There are five dimensions of Awareness of Brahma. These are explained in the subsequent verses.

I will explain the Upanisads:

1. Adhiloka Upanasad (spheres, or locations),

2. Adhijyoti Upanisad (inner Light),

3. Adhibidya Upanisad (inner Realization, or absolute Knowledge),

4. Adhipraja Upanisad (Birth, or Creation), and

5. Adhyatma Upanisad (Righteousness, or Spiritualism).

The verse deals with five point:s, location, inner Light, inner Wisdom, Creation and Consciousness.

This is called Mahasanghita, the great Scripture.

The great Scripture is explained below.

Adhilokas, or Spheres

The Earth is before, and the Sky is later.

Air, or Breath [Tranquil Breath], is the infallible means to find Adhilokas, or spheres. In other words, inside Kutastha, the inner Self between the eyebrows, there is Sky [the ethereal state of Consciousness].

By the practice of Kriya, one can enter into that Sky; the supreme Being appears as a Person inside that Sky.

Lahiri Mahasay is referring to the practice of Yonimudra. The reader must know that this particular mudra has no other name.

I am explaining (Brahma. When one holds onto the Kutastha [inner Self] with the help of tranquil intelligence, or Buddhi, this is Adhiloka, the sphere.

The earth is the first. Sign and Swaloka, or heaven, is from the navel up to Kutastha (between the eyebrows) where visions are seen. For this reason, heaven is later, and earth is first.

Birth on this earth is meant for enjoyment, and heaven is for enjoyment later. The infallible means between earth and heaven is the sky because the sky is on the earth and also in the heaven. If there were no sky, then there would be no chance for union between these two.

Between the navel and the throat is the passage to the inner dimensions of the lokas, or spheres, or places because by the practice of Air [Tranquil Breath], and through union, one can go to the Kutastha [the inner Self between the eyebrows]. This is Adhiloka.

In other words, when the Kriyanwita practices Navi Kriya, Talabya Kriya, having personally received the instructions for their practice from the Guru, or the Master, then eventually he sees the inner visions through the practice of Yonimudra.

Fire is before, and that is the first form.

At first, by the friction of inhaling and exhaling, fire is generated in the body. By this fire, all foods are digested, and the whole body remains warm.

Aditya (Kutastha: the radiant inner Self) is later. By the friction of inhaling and exhaling, the radiant Kutastha (inner Self) is seen.

In fire there is water. That is, afterwards the inner Light is seen in between the eyebrows. The water appears formless and black in color. That is, the water is the instrument or infallible clue to union.

For instance, if fire is covered by one pot with another pot, the warmth of that fire on the surface of the outer pot makes a kind of water (vapor) visible.

Similarly, the friction of inhaling and exhaling warms the head. As a result, in Kutastha [the inner Self] water appears between the eyebrows.

To find electricity, one can proceed from water through air. This is Adhijyoti, or inner Light.

There is light on the Bhu, Bhuva, and Swalokas, respectively on the coccygeal, sacral, lumbar centers.

Fixing concentration on that light, I [Sage Taitiriya] explain the Upanisad.

There is fire in all the forms of light, which are seen. For this reason, fire is first or before.

Radiant Kutastha is enjoying that which is inside and outside the earth, that is, from the navel to the leg, and from the throat to between the eyebrows (heaven, a measurement of 10 fingers).

These two lights, that is, the warmth of the body and the warmth of the inner Self, Kutastha, find their union in water.

If the fire is covered with a pot, the warmth of the pot condenses water on the surface of the pot. This water is produced by the union of the two lights. Without this water, everything would be dry, and electricity would search out the water. That electricity is in the body. That power is produced from light (fire) and water, just as the friction of the clouds produces electricity.

This is inner Light discussed in the Upanisad. By the

practice of Pranayam, that is, through the friction of inhalation and exhalation and though the practice of Yonimudra, that is, from the patches of vibration (water) in between the eyebrows, inner Light is produced.

This inner Light is enjoyed by the Kutastha, the inner Self.

Teacher is before.

The individuals, who are confused in Maya, or illusions, act in accordance with the instructions of Kutastha Brahma.

Again, Kutastha instructs the individuals how to overcome the influence of Maya and to hold onto Atma, the Self. He is the first Acharya, or teacher.

Samadhi is the result of the good practice of Pranayam and the After-effect-poise of Kriya.

To realize the state of Samadhi is called Knowledge, and this one can attain from the Guru's instructions. Thus, the personal, verbal instructions of the Guru are the infallible means to this Knowledge.

This is called sandhan, or "quest." This is Adhividya, or "absolute Knowledge." Absolute Knowledge is attained at the After-effect-poise of Kriya. Being poised in the Knowledge of the ultimate Self, I explain the Upanisad.

The Master of this Knowledge is Kutastha. As Kutastha instructs, the people accordingly perform their actions. This Adhyapaka (Kutastha), or professor, is the first teacher. So the disciple performs his actions according to Kutashta's instructions.

The Guru's [verbal] instructions are the means of attainment. The state of After-effect-poise of Kriya is attained by Kriya practice. The state of inner Realization of the ultimate Self-Knowlege reveals from Kriya practiced in accordance with the instructions of Guru.

I will explain this Wisdom, or Knowlege, of the Upanisads to you.

At first, one Eye is seen between the eyebrows by Kriya practice. Then inside the Eye, the radiant Kutastha (inner

Self) is seen. Inside Kutastha, there is Sky, and that Sky is Brahma, or the ultimate Self.

First, the Kriyanwita seeker happens to] see the inner Self everywhere; then he transcends the status of seer and seen, and the Knowledge of the ultimate Self is attained. This is called Jagya, or oblation of Prana, or the life Force.

In other words, the restless breath is offered to the tranquil Breath to attain eternal Tranquility.

Meditation is when there is a tautness in the whole body during inhalation of Pranayam. When one holds onto that state of meditation, a sound, called *Omkar*, or inner Sound, is revealed. When the mind is tranquil there, then because Brahma is seen everywhere in that Sky, meditation is automatically transcended.

Later, when the tautness affects the lower side of Apana [the life force operating below the navel], the person does not want -to speak. It is at this time when one does not speak, that automatically the breath remains in the tranquil state, and only the body and Sky remain.

When one is dissolved in that Sky, then Apana Bayu is transcended. After Prana [the breath operating between the nostril and navel], Byana [the breath throughout the body] and Apana [the breath operating below the navel] are tranquilized in Samana [the breath operating at navel].' When one stays in that Saman Bayu [life force], he begins realizing.

That [tranquil] mind itself sees Kutastha who is the greater inner Self in electricity [inner Light], which is dissolved in the Sky [the ethereal state of vibrations of the ultimate Self]. This dissolution is the transcendence of Samana.

When this Samana goes upward and Udana [the breath operating at the throat] is associated with it, then the skin [taste] is satisfied, and diseases and sufferings are removed. At this time, the air or the breath also is satisfied.

Sama means "equal," or "tranquil." Samana derives from the word Sama, which means "generality," or "universality," as well as "tranquility." Infinity is generated only in the tranquil state. Samana is the breath operating at the navel tranquilized between Prana and Apana. When the Kriyanwita is established in Samana, he sees the supreme Being in between the eyebrows by the practice of Pranayam and Navi ("navel") Kriya.

Diseases start when the air of breath is unbalanced.

So, dissolution of air [breath] in the Sky [between the eyebrows] provides the state of equilibrium Consciousness. When Brahma stays in that equilibrium state, then all are satisfied, and the Knowledge of absolute Self, or the pure Consciousness, is realized.

When by Kriya practice the Kriyanwita seeker holds onto the After-effect-poise of Kriya, he remains attuned with the state of Equilibrium resulting in eternal Tranquility.   And at that time there are no "bhabarogas, " or worldly diseases. In other words, there are no restless c/zaracter of the mind, attachments and ignorance. This is called "Adhividhya, " or Self-Knowledge.

**Without Mother there cannot be a child. So the
Mother is first, or before.**

Later, if the mind [restless breath] of the father does not go the mother, there cannot be a child; thus, the father is later.

Praja [pra, or "perfectly"; ja, "to be produced"] is to be born by oneself perfectly. Pratijanan ("birth") means to be born of oneself through the womb of his wife. This is Adhipraja, "the instrument of birth."

Having attained, or mastered, the birth, I now explain the Upanisads.

The Mother is before and the father is later, and Praja is the one who is born.

Prajanan is the Kriya of the couple which is the infallible means of the birth of the child. This is the explanation of the Adhipraja Upanisad.

**The lower palate [Nimna Talu] is first or before, and
upper palate [Uchha Talu] is later. The palate should
be in the throat [Kantha kupa].**

In other words, the tongue should be placed in Khecharimudra by the practice of Talabya Kriya. Talabya is adjective of the word Talu, or "palate."

In this way, one is beyond speech, so transcending speech (energy) is the means of Union.

Raising of the tongue [by the practice of Talabya Kriya] is the infallible means to enter into the passage of higher Consciousness.

Holding onto the ultimate Self, I am explaining the Upanisads.

The exercise of lower palate is first or before, and the exercise of upper palate is later, that is, the tautness from throat to upper palate is produced later. Transcending speech is the means of Union, then, one hears the distant sound, or develops *clairaudience.*

The tongue is the infallible means to enter into the higher Consciousness, because through the tongue speech is produced. This is the explanation of the Adhyatma [spiritual] Upanisad.

The Mahasanghita, "the great scripture, " is explained above in the light of Kriya.

The practice of different Kriyas which can be known from the Guru personally are mentioned here in brief They are as follows.‘

1. When it is said that air or breath is the infallible clue or means of seeing the supreme Person in between the eyebrows, it means to practice Kriya, or Pranayams.

2. The practice of Yonimudra, or Inner Beatific Revelation Kriya, aids the seeker in seeing the inner Light and the Black Star of Consciousness which appears like water in between the eyebrows and is the infallible clue or means of achieving inner Realization.

3. The practice of Navi Kriya, or electronizing Kriya, helps with inner Realization.

4. The practice of Omkar Kriyas and Thokar Kriyas
   (Electromagnetizing Kriyas and
   Cosmo-electromagnetizing Kriyas) helps the Kriyan-
   wita seeker to realize absolute Knowledge.

The Breath of the father becoming restless between the
eyebrows through the mother finds the passage of birth to
Creation (the restless breath is Creation).

Apparently there is manifestation, while in fact, there is
no new manifestation, since the breath, the father himself
is born through his own wife.

In the ultimate sense, only the ultimate Self in the form of
Breath, is there in all three: the father, the mother, and
the son.

**The practice of Talabya Kriya, or Khecharimudra,
that is, Inner-Outer- Space Kriya, helps towards
higher Consciousness when the tongue is put in the
Khechari. Only then, does the seeker acquire the
capacity for clairvoyance and clairaudience, and he
finds the passage to inner Realization. It is very
essential to master for achieving higher
Consciousness.**

**Whoever knows the infallible means of this
Mahasanghita, or the great scriptures, goes to the
heaven and attains Bliss.**

The Knowledge of Adhiloka, or the spheres, enlightens
the seeker to be inspired to practice Kriya in a righteous
way.

4.4 Advice Four

**Medha means "tranquil Intelligence," which is
attained after practicing Kriya or Pranayam one
hundred forty four times, perfectly according to the
Master's instructions with the tranquil Air, or
Breath.**

Then he is united with Sri [in Oneness with beatific
Energy] and becomes powerful.

A powerful person can accomplish whatever he desires.

Being transcended or dissolved at the After-effect-poise of Kriya, all become One, the ultimate Self.

In the fourth advice, all these constitute thirteen Mantras [syllables which save the mind from developing attachments], and one attains the state of After- effect-poise of Kriya through Ahuti, "the oblation."

The meaning of these Mantras comes from the Gayatri, or the Energy of Brahma, that is, the consort of Brahma, the Mother of Knowledge.

When one holds onto Gayatri, the individual self is satisfied. For this reason, self is called Madhu, or "honey." This Madhu, or honey, is the juice of all juices. Therefore, it is called "Nectar."

When the self is dissolved in the ultimate Self, it is called the state of Eternity. Whatever is said from that state becomes the word of Truth. Therefore, the first Nectar is the supreme Self.

There was nothing before the ultimate Self because it is not possible to know whether anything existed or not beyond It. And that which is not possible to know amounts to nonexistence, so it is not important.

The Nectar which was inside the body as Kutastha, the inner Self, is achieved before one receives Kriya initiation. As Kutastha was not realized, so, it was not 'important to the seeker although Kutastha was existent.

From this untruth the Truth is revealed through practicing Kriya. Kutastha, the inner Self is revealed and realized eventually.

This is the divine scheme made by the supreme Self, Himself. In other words, when the self practices Kriya of the Self, the Kutastha, the inner Self is revealed.

It is the same for the five elements [*Panchamahabhuta* earth, water, fire air and ether], which are subject to realization through the practice of Kriya Yoga.

In the beginning of inner Realization of this Kutastha Brahma (inner Self), six types of Chhanda, or "Rhythms" are revealed [in between the eyebrows], as for example, the round eye and its patches.

Later, Kutastha is revealed. Inside the Kutastha, a Star is revealed which is described as Guha, or a "cave." When one enters into that cave [by the practice of Yonimudra], one sees the greater Kutastha, where there is dazzling. radiant Light as though being produced by billions of fires, electricities, suns and moons.

Inside that extremely dazzling radiant Light reveals a throne made of Diamond on which the greater Kutastha is seen. In the greater Kutastha, the supreme Being, Lord Narayana, is seen, surrounded by Narada, Vasistha and other Sidhhas [realized sages].

There are two kinds of realizations:

1. The above described [inner Visions on the relative plane producing relative realizations].

2. The state of Oneness with Brahma, the ultimate Self, at the After-effect-poise of Kriya, or Avyakta Vidya, "inexplicable Realization [eternal Realization]." ,

Holding onto these two kinds of Realizations, the momentary divine Love is revealed.

The first is steadfast divine Love.

The second is remaining in that steadfast Love.

The third is to accept Brahma, the ultimate Self, as Lord holding onto that Love.

The Eye [the Third Eye in between the eyebrows] which is a sense, is the Karta, or subject of these three. Let Parameswara, "the supreme Being," protect me. Oh Lord God Brahma! You are the form or manifestation of this universe.

Whoever holds onto Himself attains Eternity, that is, he attains the state of Tranquility spontaneously by Kriya practice.

Let devotion be generated in my body to receive that eternal Tranquility. Let my tongue remain on the Nectar [through the practice of Talabya Kriya] which secretes at the After-effect-poise of Kriya.

Holding onto Brahma, the ultimate Self, let me listen through clairaudience. I pray all these because, the cause of all is the pure Consciousness, and he who is the Cause of all causes, stays in the cell of Power, or Energy. Since He is not fully present in my Tranquil Intelligence, I pray:

Oh Lord Kutastha Brahma! May I never forget what I have heard secretly from the mouth of the Guru, Kriya of the Self.

Let Sri, or "the inner Beauty," which is my garment, be multiplied.

Let there be always Kriya practice in this physical body, like churning a cow, and let me be enriched with the food, Brahma, the ultimate Self.

Let all the pores of my "animal body fill up with Brahma, the pure Consciousness of the ultimate Self, because being in Oneness with the ultimate Self is the transcendence, or dissolution, that is, Swaha, or "oblation."

When the Kriya is practiced, and the Kriyanwita seeker holds onto Brahma, the ultimate Self, the mind, or, the restless character of the mind is saved from being attached with outward attention.

Let those Brahmacharis whose minds are dissolved in Oneness with the Brahma, come to my house. In other words, let me see all through inner Sight.

Let those Brahmacharis come whose coming will dissolve the worldly network. That is, when all Chhandas, or Rhythms are revealed, inside, then the outside [external world] appears to be false.

By their appearance, that is, by the revelation of realized sages in between the eyebrows, reputation and welfare [enrichment in Righteousness] generate [in the Kriyanwita seeker]. [The Kriyanwita's] strength is increased, [so that he may] enter into inner Realization, Powers, and divisions of action which are made according to Providence.

Since you are all-pervading, by holding onto you all my

[the seeker's] sins will be pardoned. Like the rains which come after stormy season, the external mind [the outward attention of the mind which truly is the sin] is dissolved.

Oh Bidhata! Lord of Providence! Let such Chhandas, or rhythms, and Brahmacharis, or sages come to me. [Let such Sages reveal within me in the inner Body].

Oh Lord Brahma, ultimate Self! You are in everything and everything is within you. For this reason, your name is Pratibes, "neighbor." I request, please keep me within you.

The verses deal with the conclusion of the places, that, all are in Brahma, the ultimate Self. The seeker prays for all the righteous vibrations, beatific Revelations to be generated within him so that his animality, outward attention of mind, the sins and attachments will be removed, and he can be One with the ultimate Self.

4.5 Advice Five

On Adhijyoti: Inner Light

Bhu is measured as fifty fingers [of one's own] from the toes to the navel.

Bhuba, that is, from the navel to the throat, is measured as twenty-four fingers [of the seeker's body].

Swa, that is, from the throat to the eyebrows, is measured as ten fingers [of the seeker's body].

These three (Bhu, Bhuba and Swa) are called Brahriti, the places where the inner Realization or Knowledge of Brahma, the ultimate Self, can be attained. Brahriti are of two types:

1. Brahriti ("places"), and

2. Mahabrahriti ("great places")

Brahriti has been discussed before.

Mahabrahriti covers the rectum [genital area], navel, chest [dorsal center], the throat and the area in between the eyebrows. At the chest is Maha, If one stays there, he realizes:

Sarbang Brahma-mayang Jagat.

"The whole world is the manifestation of Brahma, the ultimate Self."

This is Mahaloka, the great place. One is Maha, the great, that is, the seer, at this fourth place [fourth from the coccygeal center], attaining the realization of Oneness between Brahma, the ultimate Self and Jagat, the universe.

At this state, the individual self becomes the great Self. However, the many gods revealed in between the eyebrows at this state are all manifestations of the supreme Self.

When the seeker practices the Kriyas, Omkar Kriya and Yonimudra, he sees through the inner Light the inner Beatific Revelations of the supreme Self in between the eyebrows which is the screen of cosmic subjective Telescope.

He sees the revelations of the Mahatma, the great Self, and, as a result, he realizes Oneness between the supreme Self and the world.

Bhu is of four kinds:

First, by the friction of the Kriya practice, one kind of fire is produced. That fire is the warmth of the body, which is from the toe to navel.

Later, from the navel to throat, thereafter, from the throat up to the eyebrows where Kutastha Brahma, inner Self, stays.

The same fire or energy dissolving at the After-effect-poise of Kriya is Bhuloka.

Second, Fire is the warmth of the body. This energy consists of three types:

1. The energy that expands and contracts operated between the rectum and penis.

2. The energy from the navel to the throat, by which, sixteen types of sounds are uttered.

3. The energy from throat to the eyebrows by which ten types of sounds and six types of inner Lights are seen.

The Light of all lights is the ultimate Self, from which all lights come, and He is the state of After-effect-poise of Kriya. This Fire or Energy is Bhu.

Third, at the state if Richa, that is, when the air remains tranquil from the eastern side of the rectum up to the navel, the seeker sees Brahma, the ultimate Self in all things. When the same air remains tranquil from the throat up to the eyebrow, then the seeker attains the state of inexplicable Brahma, the ultimate Self through *Unmani Dhyana*, or deep meditation.

Fourth, Prana, the life Force, being attracted by the Apana (air operating below the navel) to hold onto the Self in Tranquility at the navel, is Prana Brahma (Energy-Self).

When the same Prana, the life Force, operates from the navel up to the throat and is tranquil at the heart, he becomes Mahat Brahma the Great Self He is called Iswara, or God.

When the air is tranquil from the throat to the eyebrows then one inexplicable power arises and by the Power, inner Realization is achieved, and suddenly all is known.

These are the four types of Bhu in this body.

Bhuba is of four kinds: Antariksha (Ethereal), Bayu (air), Samana and Apana.

First, the tranquil Breath which generates from the navel to the throat during the time of sexual intercourse with one's wife is born. The atom of Kutastha [the inner Self], that is, the supreme Person, Himself, is born through the womb of the wife.

Second, by that air, the head, heart, and the area from the navel to the legs and all limbs are produced.

Third, with the help of Tranquil Air, the Samana air moves in all limbs in the head, navel, legs and other organs of the body.

Fourth, that air from the rectum tries to pull down Prana from the heart, and ram: from the heart tries to attract Apana upward. Thus, by this tug-of-war, the action becomes balanced, or tranquil, in the head.

Swa is of four kinds:

1. Dyuloka,

2. Aditya (Radiant),

3. Jajungsi and

4. Byana.

First, is Dyuloka. When the air is tranquil at the head, heart and navel, it is seen as Sky.

Second is Aditya. These Radiant (Adityas) are of three kinds:

1. Kutastha in between the eyebrows and tranquility at the heart;

2. Great Kutastha in the head during Yonimudra; and

3. The [round-shaped] sun without rays in the rectum.

Third, *Jajungsi* is the dazzling inner Light which is like the twelve suns at the heart, the rising of billions of suns at the head and the white sun at the rectum.

Fourth, Byana is the life Force, or air, which results in the After-effect-poise of Kriya when it goes to the head.

When it becomes tranquil at the heart, it goes throughout the body, and when it goes to the navel, it becomes tranquil.

Maha is of four kinds: Aditya (Sun), Chandrama (Moon), Brahma (ultimate Self), Paramabidya (Supreme Knowledge).

First, Aditya (Sun) is of three types:

1. Revelations of the Sun at the heart by which everything is realized.

2. Revelations of the world as Brahma (the ultimate Self) in the head as the radiant Sun.

3. Revelations of all bodies to be like suns when the air is at the navel.

Second, Chandrama (Moon) is of three types:

1. A revelation in the heart like the moon through which Peace is attained.

2. Holding onto the head with tranquil Breath which results in a revelation like the rays of the moon and is like the secretion of nectar.

3. A revelation like the moonlight in the dark at the navel which penetrates all the obstructions of the gross eye.

Third, Brahma, ultimate Self, is realized in three forms:

1. When the ultimate Self is revealed in the heart, then the atom of the ultimate Self is also revealed by which the seeker can go to all places.

2. When the ultimate Self is revealed at the navel, then the seeker attains Tranquility, and he acquires the Power to enter into all things.

3. When the ultimate Self is revealed in the head, then the seeker attains the transcendent Tranquility at the After-effect-poise of Kriya which is absolutely inexplicable. These are the three forms of revelation and realization of the ultimate Self.

Fourth, absolute Knowledge is attained in three ways:

1. When the seeker stays at the heart, and all of a sudden he attains the eternal Realization of the inner Self at the After-effect-poise of Kriya.

2. When the seeker stays at the head and he realizes amazing infinite dimensions of Consciousness.

3. When the seeker stays at the navel and he realizes Time, that is, Manifestation.

In this physical body which is *Omkar*, or inner Sound, all the Powers of absolute Knowledge, or eternal Realization, are attained.

When the seeker stays continually in that state of Realization, or Knowledge, then he attains eternal Tranquility (Lord Siva).

This Lord Siva is Brahma (the ultimate Self) in food, and all other part and gods (Devatas) are His manifestations.

The self of all parts is the radiant Sun (Aditya), and Bhu, Bhuba and Swa are the parts of the Radiant Swa of Consciousness (Aditya). That is, Bhu, Bhuba and Swa are produced from the Kutastha (the inner Self).

In the great Sky inside the heart, there is revelation which is like moonlight through which the energy of this body, air and the revelation of Kutastha (inner Self) are revealed.

I am speaking about the results of absolute Realization, or Knowledge, of the ultimate Self (Sada Siva Brahma), that is, Rik, Sama, Yaju, or in other words, the Breath of East, West, and South, and Prana and Apana, Byana of Energy of Brahma, the ultimate Self, generated through food.

Whoever knows Bhu, Bhuba, Swa and Maha by the Kriya practice realizes Brahma, ultimate Self.

Who is this ultimate Self, Brahma?

All the sages and Devatas, or gods try to realize this Brahma, or the ultimate Self.

I am speaking again for the importance to have grim Faith: Bhu, Bhuba, Swa, and Maha these two Brahriti (the places where the Knowledge of the ultimate Self can be received). These should be realized.

Generally, in Yoga Science, Mahabrahriti (spreading over) is referred to in the six centers as coccygeal (earth), sacral (water), lumbar (fire), dorsal (air), cervical (ether), sacral (water), lumbar(fire), dorsal (air), cervical (ether) and the medulla (atom of Consciousness) where the Consciousness is realized.

But Brahriti (spread over) is Bhu (the earth element: that is, the coccygeal center), Bhuba (the water element: that is, the sacral center) and Swa (the fire element: that is, the lumbar center).

Bhu means earth or the coccygeal center of the state of Brahriti. Its effect is spread throughout the body by the four different types of inner Light.

Similarly, Bhuba is not only connected with the sacral center, but its effect is spread throughout the body by the four different ways of inner Light.

Again, Swa is not only connected with the lumbar center, but its effect is spread throughout the body by the four different ways of inner Light.

Thus, at every center the inner Realization Patanjali's eightfold steps (Yama, Niyama, Asana, Pranayam, Pratya-har, Dharana, Dhyana, Samadhi which respectively mean: restraint rules, steadfast sitting, tranquil Breath, interior-ization of senses, glimpse of Tranquility, Meditation and Attunement) all of which are being realized everyday by the Kriya practitioner.

They may not be aware of it. But it is there. All these steps simultaneously remain present in everyday's prac-tice. It is a matter of awareness and attunement with love and respect.

4.6 Advice Six

I am advising on the ancient Yoga Science.

In the sky of the heart there is a person like the Sky. He is full of Mind. He is like Nectar produced out of Rik, Sama, Yaju and Atharva. He is established.

When the seeker adopts his shelter in the Sky (from the navel up to the uvula), this pure Being is revealed. The character of this pure Being is radiant, tranquil like Nectar, and ethereal like the cosmic Being.

When the air of four sides unites [by the practice of Omkar and Thokar Kriyas with the help of Talabya Kriya on the background of tranquil Breath] and adheres in between the navel and uvulla, then the radiant nectar like a tranquil, ethereal, cosmic, pure Being is seen.

That air which remains there for a while, returns to the toes or legs, again goes back to the Kutastha (inner Self betwen the eyebrows) and becomes Brahma, the ultimate Self, in the form of Energy, water and food. That state is Nectar, or Tranquility.

He who is described in Mundaka Upanisad is Lord Siva. (He who realizes the pure Self by practicing Kriya sees the pure and tranquil Self in the dazzling inner Light, the Light of all lights.)

When by the practice of Pranayam, Omkar Kriyas, coupled with Talabya Kriya, the air of the four sides of the body (Rik, Sama, Yaju, and Atharva - the four Vedas) are united and are tranquilized between the navel up to the medulla, then the radiant pure Being (Hirannoy Purusa) is seen in between the eyebrows.

He is Lord Siva who represents eternal Tranquility, that is, Equilibrium, the pure State of Consciousness of the ultimate Self.

He is seen in the dazzling inner Light of the Self which is the Light of all Lights.

Bhu: It is said first that Bhu is the loka, or place, and secondly in this Bhuloka, there is fire. So fire is said to be Bhu [a rhythm of Consciousness], and its regions are from the toe up to the navel (measuring fifty fingers).

Bhuba: First, Bhuba is subtle, and secondly it is air. So in the subtle there is air. Therefore, air can be called Bhuba, its region converging from the navel to the dorsal center. The measurement of this area, or Bhubaloka, totals twenty-four fingers: twelve fingers from the navel to the dorsal center, and an additional three fingers from the dorsal center, and nine fingers from here to the throat.

First, *Swa* is the place of tuning, secondly, it is the place of seen where there is Aditya, or the Sun, that is Kutastha (the inner Self). In other words, from the throat to between the eyebrows is measured ten fingers.

Thus, the person's body is eighty-four fingers in measurement.

First, Maha (great) is Brahma (ultimate Self), and secondly, it is Aditya (the Sun). Therefore, Maha is called Brahma, the ultimate Self.

Everybody should worship to realize this ultimate Self. Thereby one can attain one's own sentiment. That is, one can master one's own senses to become Master of the Mind.

In other words, Brahma is the Master of Tranquility, or the Moon, where there is neither light nor dark. At that time both [the mind and Brahma] become one Consciousness. That is, "I am Brahma," or the individual self, enters in Oneness with the ultimate Self.

The fire is the Master of speech or the mouth; the sun is the Master of vision or the eye; the sky is the master of audience or the ear and Iswara, or God, is the master of the science of Realization.

This is Maha or great at the After-effect-poise of Kriya what is said above.

How is this great Brahma?

In this body, which is described as ethereal Brahma or cosmic Self. He lives in this body in the Sky at the inner heart. If that ethereal-sky-Body is Brahma or the ultimate Self, then why is there supreme Knowledge of the ultimate Self? How is that supreme Person?

Satyatma Pranarama: True self is the essence of Prana, etc. Sat or Truth which is Brahma, adheres in all things. Since Truth is in all things, He is in this body also. So this body is also Truth. The body is made of five elements (earth, water, fire, air, and ether). They are five Persons like Brahma. They are also Truth. Their beginning and end are also Truth.

Sat (Existence) and Tat (Thou) that is, Satya (Truth) and Amrita (Nectar) are four signs of the Truth.

Know perfectly that Prana is the true Self. Beyond whichever Sky is described is Kutastha, who is cosmic in character. So, He is called Byomkes. (Byom means "ether" or "sky").

His other name is Risava. He is described in the Brihadaranyak Upanisad as one who plays in the body disinterestedly.

Bachang dhenumuparsita tasya Rasava manobatsa iti.

Practice Kriya (Risava means "to go"). After the practice of Kriya, the mind will be tranquil on Prana.

The Chhandagya Upanisad says,

Bagboi Gayatri.

Speech, that is, energy is Gayatri. In other words, Gayatri is the mother of Knowledge of the Veda.

When the mind and Prana become tranquil, the energy of Gayatri generates."Apa [water] and Anna [food] take the form of Kutastha. He, Himself is Mind; this is Self, full of Mind.

This is the advice. In this mind when Bliss is felt, He is called Anandamoy [full of Bliss].

The source of restless mind is the tranquil Breath.

Santi Samridhyang Santi

When restlessness ceases, the state of Santi [Peace] called Amrit [Nectar] arrives. When this is attained, death cannot touch the seeker.

This is the ancient Yoga Science. All should practice it to attain their own empire of happiness. This is called Bhava [addiction].

Counting *sa andya* [letters], etc., up to the end of Bhuba Bayu, or air, is ten.

Making sa and Aditya [Sun] the end of Amrita [Tranquility] is ten. The uniting of all is One. This totals twenty-one.

The human body can be measured by its own fingers, its length being eighty-four fingers. In it resides the cosmic inner Self, the ultimate Existence, or the pure Consciousness of the ultimate Self, which can be realized by Kriya practice abandoning the expectations for results.

4.7 Advice Seven

The Interpretation of Inner Light

I explain the Upanisads while holding onto the ultimate Self (Brahma), who is the Source of all gods and beings and the Light of all lights.

All the beings are sheltered by the inner Light. I explain the Upanisads while being one with the inner Light and with the gods of all beings (Brahma, the ultimate Self).

All beings are composed of earth, water, fire, air and ether. After the ether, there is the great subtle ether, and that very subtle ether is the Essence of all beings.

The Star, gods and great Kutastha (inner Self) are the great Beings. Even in them the same Brahma (ultimate Self) resides.

Having practiced Kriya and attained the After-effect-poise of Kriya is also Brahma (the state of Tranquility). All these three unite to become Brahma, beings, and inner Lights.

Thereafter, that inner Light inhering the self becomes Spiritual. That Self being tranquil at Samana air dissolves in Prana (life Force). When Prana dissolves in Brahma, then all the senses including taste dissolve into Brahma.

When the senses dissolve in Brahma, then the skin, the marrow and everything dissolves in the ultimate Self. That whole manifestation of Brahma is a supreme Person, from whom all these beings composed of the five elements (earth, water, fire, air, and ether) come.

Realizing that supreme Persons, Sage Taitiriya said,

Idang pangktang Sarbang

"All these are Brahma."

The spiritual aspects of four Brahriti (places) are in dissolution in one Brahma, the ultimate Self, and the After-effect-poise of Kriya.

Sage Taitiriya said,

All are in the supreme Being and all have come into manifestation from the supreme Being.

4.8 Advice Eight

The Inner Light dissolves in Inner Sound

This body which is the form and manifestation of OM, the inner Sound, is Brahma, the ultimate Self.

What is the meaning of OM? OM, the inner Sound is Brahma [the absolute Self].

I explain how this OM is Brahma. OM has become these things and in all the three lokas [places] whatever becomes is a manifestation of OM.

Thus, all are OM, inner Sound. How can it be heard? Omkar is the Sound.

I tell you how it can be heard. OM is vibrating and is secreting. What the Kriyanwitas listen to by the practice of Omkar Kriyas [inner Sound] is OM.

Who can sing this song? The followers of the Sama Veda, following the sound of OM, sing and chant hymns.

Who can adore this OM? All the holy scriptures are OM [inner Sound]. By practicing Kriya and listening to the sound of OM, people live long.

Which type of sound does it make? Following the sound of OM [inner Sound] by the practice of Omkar Kriya, the

Kriyanwita understands the tranquil Breath. One who stays in OM attains the power of clairaudience, and whatever he desires automatically is created.

Agnihotris [those who offer food or Breath to Agni, or "the god of fire," that is Kriyanwita seekers], knowing the Omkar, honestly speak of whatever they realize.

Brahmana becomes Brahma by speaking about OM, and by the practice of Kriya, he attains the stable state of Tranquility.

Therefore, he speaks always about OM and practices Kriya.

One who attains the Realization of Brahma is Brahmana.

If a mistake is made in chanting the Veda, OM should be chanted again. OM.

The inner Light finds the passage of the inner Sound OM by the practice of Omkar Kriyas.

In fact, OM is the first step of manifestation from the ultimate Self the Source of all manifestations. For that reason, the dissolution of manifestation through Kriya practice finds its passage through inner Light, and finally through the inner Sound Nada.

Through the OM, the inner Sound, the seeker attunes himself with the ultimate Self in Oneness, as the sound of OM eats the restless breath and results in Tranquility eternally.

As it is said, the essence of education lies in the proper chanting of hymns.

In other words, the chanting involves mastering the inner Sound which consists of the real vibrations in the form of rhythms and inner Light behind those letters of hymns.

In the Sanskrit alphabet the odd and even numbers contain smaller and greater degrees of energy. A particular hymn reflects a collective energy which is generated by its letters, the degree of energy depending on the position of the letters.

So, the whole spirit of education depends on attaining the

egoless state of Consciousness through chanting, that is, through the practice of Omkar Kriyas, and this chanting centers around OM (AUM).

A stands for creation or Manifestation: Lord Brahma is in charge.

U stands for endurance or sustenance of that manifestation: Lord Visnu is in charge.

M stands for dissolution of that manifestation, or absorption to Tranquility, Unmanifestation, Equilibrium. Lord Siva is in charge.

Thus, through OM (AUM), the seeker attains the state of Tranquility, or Peace.

4.9 Advice Nine : On the Adhividya

The Supreme Science or Knowledge

In the supreme Science, the Kutastha [inner Self] reveals first, and the absolute Knowledge, which is realized in Kutastha, reveals later.

The dialogue told herein is the infallible clue to inner Realization.

Swadhyaya [the study of the Self], practicing Kriya, and initiating into Kriya are all Brahmajagya [the worship of the ultimate Self].

What is seen through inner beatific Revelation Kriya, and ultimately realized, is described in the Veda.

To propagate these teachings is Dharma [real religion].

In fact, only Kriya is Truth. Speaking about Kriya with examples and listening about Kriya are the true advice of Truth.

Practicing Kriya to be in Oneness with the ultimate Self is called *Tapa* [austerity], and by this the seeker can attain the state of spontaneous Happiness, heaven and Nectar in the throat.

That is Tapa (austerity). That is Tapa (austerity).

This has been repeated twice just to conclude the advice.

The following activities such as eating ghee [clarified butter] increase longevity and strengthen the householders:

1. Agnihotra [oblation to Agni, the god of fire, or preparing food or Kriyas to offer to Kutastha],

2. Atithi seva [serving the guests],

3. Putrotpadan [producing sons],

4. Adhyayana [study],

5. Adhyapana [always holding on to the Self],

6. Educating one's son,

7. Arranging the marriage one's son,

8. Helping one's son to realize the Truth, or ultimate Self,

9. Engaging one's son in the practice of Kriya,

10. Helping one's son to hold onto the supreme Self, and

11. Holding onto Bliss.

All these are mentioned in this advice. The central point of attaining absolute Knowledge or eternal Realization is in practicing Kriya in a righteous way, that is abandoning the expectations for the results of practice.

Thus, the Kriyanwita seekers realize the Kutastha (the inner Self between the eyebrows) and eventually attain Oneness with the ultimate Self.

This is absolute Realization which is eternal, as opposed to relative realization and the transitory experiences of life.

After realizing the Self, the seeker engages himself in initiating others into Kriya, which is real propagation of religion, producing a son to continue his lineage and arranging for this sons 's marriage, achieving realization through righteous Kriya practice (Pranayam), remaining engaged in practicing Kriya and serving guests.

All these are duties and activities of the person in life.

4.10   Advice Ten

This Veda [Knowledge] was realized by the Sage Trisanku. Whatever he realized was known through this advice.

What is Veda? To know and to realize that I have become all these, that is, the entire manifestation, is Veda.

To cut the attachment or identification between the body and me by sincere Kriya practice and to attain the state of attunement (Samadhi) at the After-effect-poise of Kriya is the only means to realize this Veda.

Fear, ignorance, attachment and worldly vibration are generated due to the identification between the self (I) and body, that is, between the Spirit or Consciousness and the transitory body.

To destroy this fear is to achieve the fearless state, or absolute Freedom.

In other words, to achieve absolute Knowledge or eternal Realization by Kriya practice is the only righteous way.

The glory of the absolute Self, "I," is Mount Meru, representing eternal Existence.

The glory of the absolute Self is the cause of the entire manifestation, or divine play, eternal Existence and Bliss.

The semen of the loving husband takes birth in the wife's womb, and the child's birth and death are not possible to observe.

Similarly, the supreme Person is not seen with the gross eyes, but He is seen between the eyebrows by Kriya practice if one gets inside the high Way (Spinal Cord).

That is, by the practice of Kriya, food transforms into Brahma, the ultimate Self. Prana [life force], Mind, Satyaloka [sphere of Truth] and Amrita [Nectar or Tranquility] are gained.

At that state, living with Kutastha (the inner Self between the eyebrows), the seeker achieves inner Realization of the ultimate Self.

Thereafter, that food is Brahma (that is, Kutastha Brahma).

When that food adheres in all these, then by the action or Kriya one receives Amrita, or Nectar, that is, Tranquility. (In other words, at the After-effect-poise of Kriya the mind becomes purified from the outward attention and does not go outward.)

For that reason, in this physical body the tree of Life as I is pure at the After-effect-poise of Kriya, who is the supreme Self as I AM.

The supreme Self is not seen by the gross eyes, but can be seen in between the eyebrows when one attains the state of higher vibration through sincere Kriya practice, taking the breath inside the Spinal Cord up to the eyebrows.

That is, the practice of Kriya leads a person to the After-effect-poise of Kriya where all become One.

When all become One, this is Equilibrium, or Tranquility, which purifies all outwardness, and where the Self is established in Oneness with the ultimate Self as "I AM."

This is Amrita, or Nectar, that is, eternal Tranquility, or Bliss.

> **There is Energy of Brahma, or the ultimate Self, within me like the liquid substance, which can be taken wherever one wants.**

Pure Consciousness of the ultimate Self is natural Awareness, Bliss, and It is all-pervading.

Inhaling within me is Amrita, or Nectar, because, with the help of that inhaling, I hold onto Brahma, or the ultimate Self. That is, I see Brahma everywhere.

Breath is the essence of Eternity and is the infallible clue to attain eternal Tranquility, or eternal Realization.

One will realize Brahma everywhere when one is in Oneness with the ultimate Self within. Only then, one can see the Self everywhere.

One sees according to one's own state.

If the seeing eyes are gross, one will see nothing but gross forms. But if the eyes are assisted by lenses, then, one will see fine things like bacteria. But if the mind is taken as the eye, then, one will see subtle things.

So one sees according to the nature of the eyes.

In other words, the vibration of one's own state within causes the eyes to see accordingly.

When one is established in pure Consciousness of the ultimate Self within, one will see pure Consciousness of the ultimate Self everywhere.

4.11   Advice Eleven

To take Kriya instruction from Guru or the Master is called advice.

One who witnesses all of manifestation, is the eternal Being, Guru, or the Master. I relate to you whatever He advises.

Acharya (Guru) is Kutastha. Realizing the Kutastha (Brahma, the inner Self) and living with the Master is called Brahmacharya Asram (living with Guru in the hermitage to realize the Self).

Thus, when the education is completed in the hermitage, or Gurugriha, that is, "in the house of Guru," living with the Master, the student attends Samavarta [convocation].

Sama means "equal," and Varta means "descended." That is, when the seeker is established, he sees inner and outer as equal. Holding onto that state is called Grihastha Asram [household life], as that is truly a stable house.

And to enter into the household life style is the ruling and instruction of Guru, or the Master. The following are our duties:

1. to speak about Brahma, the ultimate Self,

2. to practice Kriya, and

3. to remain at the After-effect-poise of Kriya.

Practice Kriya with deep Sradhha, or respect, and not without Sradhha.

Thus, *Sri* [inner Realization], *Hri* [inner Illumination], and *Vri* [inner Beauty] are achieved automatically, and one realizes perfectly.

One who develops doubts about Kriya and its application is not holding onto the After-effect-poise of Kriya.

The Brahmana who practices Kriya and knows all the scriptures holds onto the After-effect-poise of Kriya always. He never develops such doubt.

Only the practice of Kriya will help one to remain at the After-effect-poise of Kriya.

If doubt is developed, still one should stay on the Kriya path.

When the whole world becomes Brahma, then hardship is over, and it becomes the same either to hold on or not to hold onto the ultimate Self.

Realizing this, you must stay on the path of Kriya. This worship or Kriya practice is the prime duty. Being a householder, one must practice Kriya. This is the rule of the scripture.

The first twenty-five years of life is student life according to Vedic culture.

The students are supposed to live with Guru together in his house or in the hermitage to learn proper chanting and realize the ultimate Self through Kriya practice. Then, at the end of their stay, they attend convocation. The Guru advises the students to return to their parents.

Upon returning to their parents, their marriages are arranged, and they now enter into household lifestyle for another twenty-five years.

The spiritual meaning of the first division of lifestyle of living with the Master means to live in Oneness with the inner Self (the real Master) between the eyebrows (hermitage), and when one thus establishes the equality (Sama) and harmony between the outside world and the inner world, it is called the balanced way of life (Samavarta, or convocation).

Then one enters into the balanced, harmonious state of life called household lifestyle. The stable and Tranquil, harmonious state is called true Abode, or House. Being a householder, one must continue to practice Kriya for eternal Realization.

Thus, the education, that is to learn the proper chanting (or to master the inner Sound behind the chanting of hymns), the rhythms, vibration of inner Light and to realize the ultimate Self through proper Kriya practice, is the essence of Vedic lifestyle.

This involves the personal relationship between the Guru or the Master and his disciples.

The Master concludes his advice to the student at the end of their student life, with further instruction of the household life to continue to practice Kriya for eternal Realization and to produce sons for lineage.

4.12   Advice Twelve

It is said, "Thou art you." You are the ultimate Self. This is the subject matter of education.

It is said that the inner Light is the means to get into inner Illumination and beatific Revelations. It is also said that the absolute Knowledge or eternal Realization of the ultimate Self is Truth.

Whatever you saw is the Truth. Let that Lord remain within me as the speaker.

The essence of education is to realize Brahma, the ultimate Self, which is the ultimate, eternal Existence.

He is eternal Being, the Source of all, the entire manifestations.

He is the Source of divine Love, absolute Knowledge, absolute Freedom and eternal Bliss.

Om Shanti ! Shanti ! Shanti !

Chapter 5

The Tejabindu Upanisad : The Mystic Energy

**Tejobindo parang Dhyanang biswatitang hridi
sthitang.
Anubang sambhabang santang sthulang sukshang
parancha jat.**

After one practices Pranayam, or Kriya, for 1,728 times,
the mystic Energy, or inner Light and Spot [Bindu], that
is, Kiitastha [the inner Self] is revealed beyond the world
[Biswa].

Biswa (Bi+s+wa): The word Biswa ordinarily means "world"
which represents the following in Kriya:

Bi, or Bises: "absolute way."

s, or Swa: "the individual self representing the all-pervading
Lord Siva |Tranquility]."

wa: "the Voidness in the throat beyond Omniscience at
the After-effect-poise of Kriya."

He is in the Heart of Kutastha [the area between the eye-
brows].

Anu-bang: The word Ana ordinarily means "atom, " and
it represents the following in the light of Kriya:

Anu: Brahma, the ultimate Self.

Sambhabang: Kutastha [the inner Self in between the eyebrows].

Santang: The word Santang means "Tranquility."

Santa: the gross manifestations, the all-pervading "Siva Lingam" [the oval-shaped stone worshiped as Lord Siva's penis, representing Lord Siva as personified Tranquility] in all atoms, the ultimate Self, who is the subtlest of all subtleties.

Parancha jat: Literally, "and who is beyond all manifestations."

The mystic Energy is beyond all worldliness and attachments. It is in the Heart, the area in between the eyebrows. It is called Kutastha, the inner Light.

It is attainable when the seeker of Truth, the Kriyanwita, practices Omkar/Ongkar Kriyas after having achieved the Tranquil Air by the practice of Talabya Kriya, or Khecharimudra.

The purpose of Kriya practice is not to achieve Yogic powers but eternal Tranquility (Sthirattva) through mystic Energy. The mystic Energy is automatically generated when the Breath, or Air, becomes Tranquil at the After-effect-poise of Kriya.

The aim of Kriya science is to attain the state of Santa, the eternal Tranquility at the After-effect-poise of Kriya. When the seeking self merges in Oneness with the ultimate Self, it is the state of After-effect-poise of Kriya.

The same state is in Oneness with the world, that is, when all three, the seeking self, the ultimate Self and the world, are dissolved in Oneness, then the state of eternal Tranquility (Santa, or Sthirattva) reveals or generates in the seeker. This state of Santa is eternal Bliss, or the state of beyond the After-effect-poise of Kriya.

Om Dusadhyancha Duraradhyang, Dusprekhyancha Durasrayam.
Durlakshang Dustarang Dhyanag, Muninancha Munisinam.

Dusadhyancha: Du + sadhyancha/sadhana.

Dusadhyang: "hardly attainable."

Du: "with sufferings," or "staying away from Brahma, the ultimate Self."

Sadhyanag/Sadhana: "even Kutastha is seen by the practice of Sadhana."

Although it is difficult to practice Kriyas, still by hard work [steadfast practice] the Kutastha can be seen, and the ultimate Self can be attained. That is why it is called Dusadhyang.

Duraradhyanag (Du+a+ya+ra+dhi+a):
Duraradhyang means "difficult to pray."

Du: "away from the ultimate Self, or Brahma."

a: "coccygeal center."

ya: "holding onto the coccygeal center a long time by the upward energy of the Spinal Cord."

ra: "to take up the Eye."

dhi: "Intelligence poised in inner Wisdom."

a: "to come back again to the coccygeal center."

Dusprekhyang (Du+pra+ng/m): meaning "difficult to see."

Du: "staying away from the ultimate Self, Brahma."

pra: "seeing perfectly in the Kutastha."

ma: "Medulla oblongata."

This is the Form of Brahma.

To perfectly see Kutastha, the inner Self, at the Medulla through the area between the eyebrows by the practice of Yonimudra (Beatific Inner Revelation Kriya) with the Tranquil Air, or Breath, is the Form of Brahma.

Durashrayang (Du+ashrayang/m): Ashrayam means "shelter. " Durashryam means "difficult place to hold onto. "

Ashrayam: "holding onto the Kriya practice."

a: "holding longer at the coccygeal center."

sa: "individual self."

ra: "bringing up the Eye."

a: "again bringing back to the coccygeal center."

The spontaneous state of Consciousness is Brahma, the ultimate Self. It is difficult to approach Brahma with Kriya practice with efforts until the Kriyanwita seeker achieves the After-effect-poise of Kriya through the Tranquil Breath, or Air. That is why it is called Dusprekhyang.

Durlakhyang (Du+la+kshyang/m): Kutastha is difiicult (Du) to look at (lakhyang). So it is called Durlakhyang.

Du: "staying away from the ultimate Self."

la: "by the two palates [Khecharimudra, or Talabya Kriya to be applied]."

Kshyang/m: "fixing the attention of the sight, or eyes, at the root of the eyes and nose, that is, between the eyebrows."

It is difficult to look at the Kutastha in between the eyebrows due to the dazzling inner Light without establishing oneself in Khecharimudra, or Sambhabimudra.

Dustara (D+u+ta+ra): meaning "difficult way to approach."

D: Yoni.

u: "coccygeal center," that is, pressing hard at the coccygeal center.

ta: again, "pressing forcefully at the coccygeal center."

ra: "the Eye."

The Kriyanwita seeker must find first the passage inside the Spinal Card to travel High up; otherwise, it is always difficult to arrive up to the Yoni (between the eyebrows).

Yoni means literally "place of creation," that is, "genital organs," but spiritually, Yoni means "Kutastha, " the inner Self between the eyebrows from where the individual breath, or being, is born.

Dhyanang (Dhyana): Dhyana means "meditation."

Dhyana: The Tranquility achieved by the Yogi who has

practiced Pranayam 1,728 times. Holding onto that Tranquility, he automatically becomes silent.

The state of Tranquility generated from the practice of Omkar/Ongkar Kriyas 1,728 times is called Dhyana, or meditation, in Kriya.

This verse deals primarily with the practice of Omkar Kriya with the help of the Tranquil Air, of Breath.

Moving from the coccygeal center to the eyebrows and back to the coccygeal center and practicing such Omkar Kriyas 1,728 times will completely quiet the mind, the restless breath, and the seeker will attain eternal Tranquility automatically at the After-effect-poise of Kriya. His intelligence will be poised in inner Wisdom (absolute Silence), and automatically he will become a saint, a Mauni Swami, or Baba.

> **Om jitaharo jitakrodho, jitasango jitendriya.**
> **Nridwando nirahangkaro, Nirasiraparigraha.**

Jit means "mastering the senses," that is, "overcoming the influence of the senses."

Jitahara (Jit+a+ha+ra): Literally, Ahara means "food."

A: To stay in the coccygeal center longer.

ha: to be attracted longer and nourished longer by the life force, Prana Bayu.

ra: the decreasing of sight [outwardness of mind with the sentiment of seeing].

Ahara, or "food," is Breath in the light of Kriya.

Jitahara is to overcome the power of tlte senses and to hold onto the natural state at the After-effect-poise of Kriya.

Jitakrodho (Jit+k+r+o+dha): Krodha means "anger."

K: "head."

r: "the Eye."

o: "the Spot (Bindu)."

dha: "Intelligence."

Looking at something with attachment while holding onto it in the head and trying to see into its atom is the state of anger (Krodha). When this is overcome, there are no purposes or visions.

When the Kriyanwita seeker holds onto the ultimate Self turning the attention of the mind inward, overcoming the power of senses (anger), it is called Jitakrodha.

Jitasanga (Jit+sanga): Sanga means "association."

Jitasanga: Beyond desires, mastering the senses, i.e., the After-effect-poise of Kriya.

Nirdwando(Ni+dwanda): Dwanda means "conflict. "

Ni: "No."

dwanda: "hesitation," or "dualism," the relative plane.

So, Nirdwando is beyond dualism, or the ultimate Self.

Nirahangakara (Ni+ahangkara): Ahangkara means "ego."

Ni: "No."

ahangkara: "sense of ego."

So Nirahangkara is the After-effect-poise of Kriya, or eternal Tranquility, where there is no sense of ego or intellect.

Nirasi (Ni+asi): Asa means "hope" or "expectations."

Ni: "No."

asa: "expectations."

So *Nirasi* means one who has transcended the expectations of results of Kriya practice and yet who practices sincerely.

Aparigraha (A+parigraha): Paraigraha means "looking for help."

A: "No."

parigraha: "looking outward."

At the state of Aparigraha the mind does not become outward.

When the seeker by the practice of Kriyas attains the Tranquil Breath, or the Tranquil Air, then all becomes Tranquil, just One Consciousness.

The After-effect-poise of Kriya is beyond dualism and the

intellect. In that state of unique Consciousness, the mind, the ego, the intellect and thought, being unreal, simply disappear. Then pure Consciousness prevails as eternal Existence, the addiction of eternal Bliss.

Om agamya gamya karta cha Gurumanartha mamasa. Mukhani trini bindanti tridhama Hangsa uchate.

Agamya (A+gamya): Where no one can go, is the place Agamya.

A: "No."

gamya: "to go."

Where no one can go is the After-effect-poise of Kriya.

At the state of eternal Tranquility at the After-effect-poise of Kriya where everything is in equilibrium, there is no motion. So, there is no possibility of restlessness. No one can approach Tranquility with restless mind. That is why it is called Agamya.

Gamya: literally meaning "to go."

Gamya: The place where one can go, that is, do something. The responsibility lies in Brahma, the ultimate Self, that is, the Guru-Brahma at the After-effect-poise of Kriya, which is the true Form of the ultimate Self.

At the Tranquil Breath, mind, being tranquil, merges into the After-effect-poise of Kriya, where Guru and Brahma become just One.

Mukhani trini bindanti: Three kinds of Joy are felt by the individual self in the ultimate Self.

The seeking self feels Joy in the Tranquil state of Breath, the After-effect-poise of Kriya and seeing Guru-Brahma in Oneness.

Tridhama hangsa uchate: Tri means "three, " Dhama means "house," and literally Hang Sa means "swan."

Tri: "three."

dhama: "centers" : the navel, dorsal and throat.

hang: "inhaling."

sa: "exhaling."

Holding onto the ultimate Self at the After-effect-poise of Kriya is eternal Tranquility at the three centers : navel, dorsal and throat.

Holding steadfastly inside the Spinal Cord, eternal Tranquility is held by the attainment of tranquil Breath (inhaling and exhaling), which is called Hang Sa.

By the practice of Kriya through inhaling and exhaling, tranquilizing the air of breath inside the Spinal Cord, eventually crossing through the aforesaid centers, and dissolving the mind, the Kriyanwita seeker can attain eternal Tranquility.

Om parang gujyamidang sthanam avyaktam Brahma nirashrayam.
Byomarupam kalasukshang Visnostatparamang padam.

Param-gujyam: Param means "highest." Gujyam means "secret. "

Param-gujyam: Whatever is secret is seen in the inner revelations. The After-effect-poise of Kriya, which is inexplicable, is the highest secret of all.

Therefore, nothing can be said about Brahma, the ultimate Self, which is without Substratum.

He is Brahma, the ultimate Self. He Himself is Substratum of Himself. For this reason, He is called Unseen (Arupa/Arupam). But nothing except One ethereal feeling of Voidness is there.

Sixteen types of manifestations can be seen in the Moon beyond them. There are the subtle revelations where only they can be felt.

When the Kriyanwita seeker 's breath is tranquilized at the throat, the cervical center contains sixteen petals and the sixteen Letters, or Aksharas, which are associated with the sixteen petals and which vibrate in the Moon, that is, in Tranquility.

Beyond that ethereal state, the subtler revelations are felt when the Breath is tranquilized at the medulla center.

Visnutat param padam: The state of eternal Tranquility called Lord Visnu, that is, Kutastha Brahma, the inner Self.

The seeker can attain this eternal Tranquility when he remains attuned between the eyebrows. This is called highest Bliss.

To start from the coccygeal center go up to Above and back to the coccygeal center when steadfastly the same mystic Energy is Tranquil: this is the ultimate Self, Brahma, the highest Attainment.

The state of eternal Realization of the One Self which is the ultimate Existence, is supremely secret. That is the After-effect-poise of Kriya. It is a state of Consciousness which is a Unique, Equilibrium, Harmonious state.

The ultimate Self is the Source of all manifested things and, as such, is the Substratum of all, including Himself. So, the ultimate Self in fact is Formless, beyond the seen.

He can only be realized at the After-effect-poise of Kriya when the Air of Breath becomes Tranquil by the practice of Kriyas. At the Tranquil state of the Air of Breath all becomes One.

Therefore, being One with the ultimate Self and not seeing the Self, or transcending inner revelations, is eternal Realization. At that state, the whole Spine is alerted and attuned to this mystic Energy in Oneness by the practice of Omkar Kriyas.

Pure Consciousness of the ultimate Self is all inclusive; nothing is outside. It is a Blissful state.

Om Trambakang trigunang sthanang tridhatu rupa barjitam.
Niskalang niravilakpancha niradharang nirashrayam.

Trambakang (Tri + ambaka): He is the highest Happiness, or Bliss, at the three centers : navi (navel), Anahat (dorsal), and Kantha (cervical).

Trigunanag (Tri+guna): The three qualities (sattva, "divine"; rajasa, "positive"; tamasa, "negative") associated with the three currents of energy, that is, Susumna (Spine), Ida and Pingala.

The same Consciousness is in all movable and immovable beings.

Tridhatung (Tri+dhatu): Three things : bayu ("air"), pittva ("bile") and kopha ("cough") : respectively, working at navi (the navel), hridaya (the heart) and gala (the throat).

Rupabarjitang (Rupa+barjita): When Goddess Saraswati, the Goddess of Knowledge, or Realization, that is, Kundalini Energy, is covered with illusion in the three nerves, Ida, Pingala and Susumna. She is coiled at the base of the Spine. But at the After-effect-poise of Kriya she [the Kundalini, mystic Energy] is free from this coiled state.

Niskalang (Ni+kala): The outside air will remain outside the nose; the eyes will remain fixed in between the eyebrows; Prana and Apana will remain tranquil at the navel; air will flow within the nostril. When such a state is held, it is the sign of Samadhi ("eternal attunement in Oneness with the spontaneous state of Consciousness"). This is called Niskala.

Nirvikalpang (Ni+vikalpa): All present and future desire is called Kalpana, that is, "imagination," while the reverse is "no desire," called Vikalpa, that is, "rejection," or "substitution".

Therefore, the absence of both sets : no desire and desire and desire and no desire : is the state of pure Consciousness free from all thoughts, Nirvikalpa.

Niradharang (Ni+adhara): The state of Awareness upon which the establishment of Tranquility is based is called Adhara, "container."

At the state of After-effect-poise of Kriya even that sense of container (Source) is dissolved. Hence, truly it is beyond everything.

Nirashrayam (Ni+ashrayam): The state of beyond After-effect-poise of Kriya

Kriyar-para-basthar-parabastha

is without substratum, support, or shelter. That is why it is called Nirashrayam.

When the mystic Energy leaves the coiled state from the Spine, the feeling of manifold manifestations is dissolved, and the seeker enters into the state of Oneness at the tranquil state of Breath.

At that state, the air outside the body remains outside, while the tranquil Air works within the nostril inside the body on a subtle plane, as the inhaling and exhaling is at the navel, which is responsible for dragging everything from the outside and making easement from inside.

Then the attention of the eyes are fixed in between the eyebrows, and everything becomes One and is stilled into Tranquility, the state of Consciousness called Samadhi in Yoga literature.

Then when the desires, attachments and the restless character of the mind due to imagining, planning, selecting, rejecting, are all dissolved, the perfect state of pure Consciousness is achieved.

Then the seeker, in other words, the seeking self, is in Oneness with the ultimate, pure Self, the state described in yoga as Nirvikalpa Samadhi. This state of unique, marvelous Consciousness is free from attachment to thoughts. At the same time, all inclusive, nothing is separate from the ultimate Self.

When the restless breath becomes Tranquil by the Kriya practice, the manifold manifestation becomes One. This is the ultimate state of Consciousness, the ultimate Self as the Source of manifestations, as well as the melting Ground of manifold manifestations into Oneness.

Some people attempt to describe through imaginations of mind that absorbing state of Oneness as a black hole. This is an erroneous description of this state It is like saying that the reflections in the mirror which are not real, are real.

Om Upadhirahitang sthanag bangmanoyatita gocgaram.
Swavaba vabana grajyang sanghataikapadojajhitam.

Upadhi rahitang sthanang: Upadhi, "name"; rahitang, "less" or "beyond"; sthanang, "place. "

At the After-effect-poise of Kriya, the intellect is poised in inner Wisdom.

That is, intellect and thoughts are being dissolved there; individuality is merged in Tranquility, so this state cannot be named. Only Silence prevail as as Eloquence.

Bangmanotitang (Baka+mana+atita): "beyond speech and mind."

With the restless mind, the state of After-effect-poise of Kriya cannot be attained.

Gochara (Go+chara): Literally, Go means "to go " "cow " and "tongue chara means "movement."

Go: "tongue."

chara: "when raised [by the practice of Talabya Kriya, or Khecharimudra]." Only then the state of real Tranquility can be felt.

That is why Talabya Kriya is the precondition to practice Omkar/Onkar Kriyas. Without practicing Khechari, no one is able to feel Tranquility, or purity of Peace.

Swavava (Swa+vava): Swa means "oneself, " and vava means "nature. "

Swa: "Oneself," "the individual (Jiva)."

vava: "beyond the three qualities.

This is Tranquility at the After-effect-poise of Kriya.

Swavava is the natural state of Consciousness. To establish oneself in one's Swavava is to establish oneself in eternal Tranquility at the After-effect-poise of Kriya.

Grajyang: Grajya means "to accept."

Grajya: to accept Oneself by Oneself and to hold onto the state of Tranquility at the After-effect-poise of Kriya.

Practicing Omkar Kriyas and being merged in one's own eternal Self Within is called Grahan, or acceptance, another term for Oneness with the ultimate Self.

Sanghataikapadojajhita (Sanghat + Pada): "Sanghat" means "encounter" and "pada" means "state" or "leg".

Sanghata: Such confrontation is felt only when experiencing death.

pada: the state of merging into Oneness.

When the manifestation of inhaling and exhaling (the still state) is stopped in a natural course during the Kriya practice, or Pranayam, then the Air of Breath becomes tranquil. This is the actual Tranquil Air(Sthira bayu). This tranquil Air works in a subtle plane inside.

Eventually, the seeker, by practicing Omkar Kriyas with the help of Tranquil Air, will achieve the state of eternal Tranquility at the After-effect-poise of Kriya. This state is so tranquil, beyond the three qualities, that until the seeker is established in Khecharimudra, or Talabya Kriya (Inner-Outer-Space Kriya), he or she cannot achieve the state of eternal Tranquility.

The importance of Khechari, or Talabya Kriya, is tremendous. That is why it forms the essential qualification, or a stability, to practice Omkar Kriyas. In fact, Khechari brings the death to the impurities or attachments of all sensual character.

We may be reminded here that mind, intellect, and ego are also considered inner-sense organs.

In that state, the seeking self merges in the pure Self in Oneness and finds the state of pure Consciousness. This is highest Attainment, and it can be achieved only by the deathlike experiences; that is, this state of absolute Consciousness of the ultimate Self is attained only when the seeker dies or dissolves the individual consciousness perfectly.

Om Anandang nandanatitang dusprekshyang
Ajambayam.
Chitivritti binirmuktam Saswatang
Dhirubanmachyatam.

Anandang: As one is joyful when he has a son, likewise, the individual self is joyful when he finds the supreme Being always in himself. Then he goes beyond where there is even no trace of supreme Being. Thus, at the After-effect-poise of Kriya, there is no sense of Joy.

Dusprekshyang: There is no chance to see well.

Due to dazzling radiant inner Light, it becomes difficult to look at the radiant Kutastha, the inner Self.

Ajam(A+ja): A means "no" ,' Ja means "born. "

A: "No."

ja: "birth."

All the world is Brahma, the ultimate Self. If this is so, how can there be birth? When Brahma Yoni, i.e., the Source, is all there is, and there is no Siva Lingam, or individual self, at the After-effect-poise of Kriya, how can there be birth?

Avyayam (A+vyaya): *A* means "no"; *Vyayam* means "destruction."

A: "No."

vyaya: "change" or "destruction."

So Avyayam means "no change."

How could there be a change of things when there is just One Brahma, or ultimate Self?

Chitta vrittvi binir muktam: The mind being tranquil for a while in the Spot (Bindu) of the heart is called heart of Chittva.

Chitta vritti: "the waves of that heart," i.e., looking outward with attachment.

To be free from the changing of the present state is to hold always onto Brahma, the ultimate Self.

Saswatang: Perfectly established in the state of Tranquility at the After-effect-poise of Kriya, which is truly the eternal Self.

Dhrubang (Dhruba): *Dhruba*: To be established in Tranquility in the very subtle way in the atom of Consciousness is called true establishment. That is called eternally true Self

Nityang Brahmang Dhrubang

Brahmang Achyuta (A+chyuta): Chyuta means "falling apart. "

A: "No."

chyuta: "discharge, or semen."

Achyuta means that when the seeker attains Tranquility, his attention never becomes outward with attachment.

When the Kriyanwit seeker achieves the state of eternal Tranquility at the After-effect-poise of Kriya, he is in Oneness with : even beyond : the supreme Self. That is, he is just the pure Consciousness, free even from the feeling of Oneness. As such, that state is beyond the scope of the birth of individual consciousness and is essentially the one pure Consciousness of the ultimate Self beyond change and manifestation.

It is the state of eternal Tranquility, the unique, harmonious equilibrium state of pure Consciousness, the eternal Existence from which attention never becomes outward.

Om tad Brahmanang tadadhyatmang tannistha tat parayanam.
Achittachittamatmanang tadbyomam param sthitam.

Tad- Brahmang: "He holds onto the ultimate Self, Brahma."

Tad-Adhyatmang: "The poising of intelligence in inner Wisdom - that is, the attaining of the After-effect-poise of Kriya - is spiritualism (Adhyatma)."

Adhi means "Realization."

Knowledge of the Self Atma is Adhyatma, that is, spiritualism.

But what is Spirit? The word Spirit is derived from the Latin word "Spiritus" which means "Breath." So Spirit is nothing but Breath.

In other words, one can realize the spirit only when one is in the Tranquil Breath, or Tranquil Air, by the practice of Kriya. So, without practicing Pranayam, or Kriya, no one can grow to Spirit, that is, achieve eternal Tranquility.

Tan-nistha: Holding steadfastly onto [Kutastha, the inner Self] is sincerity.

Tat-parayana: To attain that state of pure Consciousness and to hold onto that state of Consciousness spontaneously is Tat-parayana.

Achitta-chitta-matmanang: Tranquility of the restless individual self in the state of After-effect-poise of Kriya is the means to silence the restless nature of the heart.

Tat-byoma: It is like the Void, that is, Brahma, the ultimate Self.

Param-sthitam: Param means "highest"; sthitam means "established."

Param-sthitam: He is beyond all, beyond which there is nothing. The eternal equilibrium state of pure Consciousness is eternal Peace.

When the seeker of Truth of the absolute Self holds onto the After-effect-poise of Kriya sincerely and switches over to the spontaneous state of Consciousness, he attains the eternal Tranquility beyond which there is nothing. This very eternal Tranquil state of unique pure Consciousness is the eternal Existence of mystic Energy (Teja).

Asunye Sunya vabang cha sunyatitam absthitam
(Hridistham).
Na dhyanang nacha ba dhyatana dhyeo dhyeya eba
cha.

Asunye-sunya-vabastha: *Asunye-sunya-vaba* means "Void without Voidness. "

Asunye+sunya+vaba: The feeling of Voidness in the Voidlessness; there is no vision of Voidness.

Sunya-titang: To hold onto the Formless state beyond Voidness attained automatically by the Kriyanwita seeker, who does not like to talk about this state.

Na+dhyanang+dhyeya+dhyata:

Na: "No."

dhyanang: "meditation."

dhyeya: "object of meditation."

dhyata: "meditator."

The state of pure Consciousness is beyond meditation (Dhyana), that which is meditated upon (Dhyeya), and meditator (Dhyata). [All three are in Oneness].

At the After-effect-poise of Kriya, in other words, in the eternal Tranquility, the unique, equilibrium state of pure Consciousness, there is no meditator, no object of meditation, and no meditation itself.

The state is beyond all. It is the spontaneous equilibrium state of eternal Silence. The holy scripture put it as eternal Peace.

Sarba tat paramang sunya na parang Paramatparam Achintam prabudhancha na cha Satyang na sangbidu.

Sarbancha-paramang-sunyang:
Above all, Kutastha Brahma is supremely Void.

Na parang paramat param: "Beyond which there is nothing supreme."

Achintang (A+chintang): *A* means "no"; *chinta* means "thought."

Achintang: "Not possible to attain through thoughts as the ultimate Self is beyond thoughts."

Satya na cha sangbidu: "Unknowable," i.e., "not possible to know perfectly." This state of pure Consciousness of the ultimate Self is the supreme state of Existence, or mystic Energy, which is beyond all thoughts. It is not attainable and understandable through thoughts and intellect anyway.

**Muninang tattwajuktantuna Deva na parang bidu
Lovang, mohang, vayang darpang, kamang,
krodhancha kilwisam.**

Muninang tattwa juktantu: "Only attainable by the Sages by means Of concentration, or one-pointed mind."

Na Deva: "Even the gods who see Kutastha cannot attain the state of eternal Tranquility."

Na parang bidu: "All lower than gods cannot know that state of supreme Consciousness either."

Lovang, mohang, vayang darpang, kamang, krodhang: "The After-effect- poise of Kriya is free from greed, attachment, fear, pride, sensual love, anger and sin.

The state of pure Consciousness, which is One, is attainable by the sincere practice of Kriyas, and not by beginners of the practice and seers of inner visions.

The state of After-effect-poise of Kriya, when all becomes just One, is free from all senses and sentiments, including the inner sense like the mind or ego.

Sitosnang khutpipasancha sankalpancha vikalpam.
Na Brahma kuladarpancha na muktigrantha
sanchayam.

Na vayang sukha dukhancha tatha manapamanayo.
Etadvabha binirmuktam tadgrajyang Brahma param.

That state of Consciousness is free from all sentiments like pride, sense Of liberation, fear, pleasure and pain, and honor and dishonor.

That state of Consciousness is the ultimate Self, i.e., the state of After-effect-poise of Kriya.

The ultimate Self, Brahma, is totally free from all sentiments whatsoever. It is the pure Consciousness, almighty Power (Teja), Wisdom (Jnana) and Freedom (Mukti).

OM. Shanti ! Shanti ! Shanti !

word uttered by a Yogi has a special meaning that is totally unintelligible to even the highly intellectual people. This book is written in such a way that everyone can follow it up while trading the path of Kriya. People think that they are very intelligent, but if they try to understand very seriously, they realize perfectly that nothing is happening according to their intellect.

Only those whose breath is not blowing in the left or right nostril are intelligent in this world.

This is a a scriptural commentary of Lahiri Mahasaya on *The Guru Gita* in the Light of *Kriya*. Lahiri Mahasaya is a polestar of Kriya Yoga, a direct disciple of Mahavataar Babaji. In previous birth, he was Kabir. He is the Sadguru of Saint Shirdi Sai Baba.

Guru Gita is a part of *Biswasar Tantra*. Divine Mother, *Parvati*, was sitting with Lord Siva, her divine husband, on Kailas Mountain in the Himalayas when she requested him to impart the great teaching of *Guru Gita* to her.

This important scripture will help the seekers of Truth to better understand and clarify the Kriya path in their pursuit of Truth:

- Who is *Guru* ?

- What is *Guruseva* (service to *Guru*) ?

- How does one meditate upon *Guru* ?

- Who is qualified to have *Kriya* ?

This book is written for preparing common mass to embrace a very simple but powerful self-help mechanism of drinking air(not breathing air) to eradicate Diabetes(both Type 1 and 2) from root and foster longevity with healthy body and mind.

These simple techniques are meant to be practiced by anyone without any external assistance and guidance.

This is a scriptural commentary of Lahiri Mahasaya on The Omkar Gita in the Light of Kriya in which God Krishna answers to Prince Arjuna about the Omkar.

Lahiri Mahasaya is a polestar of Kriya Yoga, a direct disciple of Mahavataar Babaji. In previous birth, he was Kabir. He is the Sadguru of Saint Shirdi Sai Baba.

This is a scriptural commentary of Lahiri Mahasaya on Kabir's couplets.

Lahiri Mahasaya is a polestar of Kriya Yoga, a direct disciple of Mahavataar Babaji. In previous birth, he was Kabir. He is the Sadguru of Saint Shirdi Sai Baba.

This is a scriptural commentary of Lahiri Mahasaya on The Bhagavad Gita.

1. *Bisad Yoga : Arjuna's (Seeker's) Melancholy*

2. *Sankhya Yoga : Knowledge of the Self*

3. *Karma Yoga : Action*

4. *Jnan Yoga : Knowledge and Wisdom*

5. *Karma-Sanyas Yoga : Action and Renunciation*

6. *Avyas Yoga : Practice*

7. *Jnan-Bijnan Yoga : Knowledge and Realization*

8. *Akshara-Brahma Yoga : The Eternal Self*

9. *Raja Vidya Raja Gujya Yoga : The Supreme Science and The Supreme Secret*

10. *Bibhuti Yoga : The Divine Glories*

11. *Biswarupa Darsan Yoga : The Universal Form of The Self*

12. *Bhakti Yoga : Devotion*

13. *Kshetra and Kshetrajna : The Prakriti-Purusha Yoga*

14. *Gunatraya Bibhag Yoga : Threefold Qualities*

15. *Purushottam Yoga : The Supreme Person*

16. *Daibasura Sampad Bibhag Yoga : The Divine and Demoniacal Properties*

17. *Shraddhatraya Bibhag Yoga : The Threefold Respect*

18. *Moksha Yoga : Liberation*

This is a Kriya Yoga book intended to be read and practiced by everyone, with/without initiation.

Every word uttered by a Yogi has a special meaning that is totally unintelligible to even the highly intellectual people.

This book is written in such a way that everyone can follow it up while trading the path of Kriya.

People think that they are very intelligent, but if they try to understand very seriously, they realize perfectly that nothing is happening according to their intellect.

Only those whose breath is not blowing in the left or right nostril are intelligent in this world.

When breathing is faster, then in one day and one night respiration can flow up to 113,680 times. Normally during the same time, the figure is 21,600 times. During a day and night, if respiration is faster than usual, the breath can flow in and out 113,680 times. Normally, in the course of a day and night, there are 21,600 breaths. This figure is reduced by Kriya practice to 2,000 times. So, breathing 1,000 times in the day and 1,000 times in the night, in a normal course, provides greater Tranquility to a Yogi. One of his breaths takes about 44 seconds. Such a Yogi is matured in Kriya practice.

Thoughts are inseparably related to breathing. So, when the number of breaths is reduced, thoughts are reduced proportionately. Eventually, with the tranquilization of breath, thoughts are dissolved. Thereby, the seeker can attain the After-effect-poise of Kriya, or eternal Tranquility, which is Amrita, nectar proper.

SELECTED WORKS OF LAHIRI MAHASAYA

LAHIRI MAHASAYA

This is a compilation of selected works of Lahiri Ma-hasaya.

1. The Bhagavad Gita

2. The Omkar Gita

3. The Upanishads

4. Kabir's Dohe(Couplets)

LIST OF TITLES WITH ISBN NO.

ISBN	TITLE
9788194914129	1984
9789390575220	1984 & Animal Farm (2In1)
9789390575572	1984 & Animal Farm (2In1): The International Best-Selling Classics
9789390575848	35 Sonnets
9789390575329	A Clergyman's Daughter
9789390575923	A Study In Scarlet
9789390896097	A Tale Of Two Cities
9789390896837	Abide in Christ
9789390896202	Abraham Lincoln
9789390896912	Absolute Surrender
9789390896608	African American Classic Collection
9789390575305	Aldous Huxley: The Collected Works
9789390896141	An Autobiography of M. K. Gandhi
9789390575886	Animal Farm
9789390575619	Animal Farm & The Great Gatsby (2In1)
9789390575626	Animal Farm & We
9789390896158	Anna Karenina
9789390575534	Antic Hay
9789390896165	Antony & Cleopatra
9789390896172	As I Lay Dying
9789390896226	As You like it
9789390575671	At Your Command
9789390575350	Awakened Imagination
9789390575114	Be What You Wish
9789390896233	Believe In yourself
9789390896998	Best of Charles Darwin: The Origin of Species & Autobiography
9789390896684	Best Of Horror : Dracula And Frankenstein
9789390575503	Best Of Mark Twain (The Adventures of Tom Sawyer AND The Adventures of Huckleberry Finn)
9789390896769	Black History Collection
9789390575756	Brave New World, Animal Farm & 1984 (3in1)

9789390896240	Brother Karamzov
9789390575053	Bulleh Shah Poetry
9789390575725	Burmese Days
9789390896257	Bushido
9789390896066	Can't Hurt Me
9788194914112	Chanakya Neeti: With The Complete Sutras
9789390896042	Crime and Punishment
9789390575527	Crome Yellow
9789390575046	Down and Out in Paris and London
9789390896844	Dracula
9789390575442	Emersons Essays: The Complete First & Second Series (Self-Reliance & Other Essays)
9789390575749	Emma
9789390575817	Essential Tozer Collection - The Pursuit of God & The Purpose of Man
9789390896578	Fascism What It Is and How to Fight It
9789390575688	Feeling is the Secret
9789390575190	Five Lessons
9789390575954	Frankenstein
9789390575237	Franz Kafka: Collected Works
9789390575282	Franz Kafka: Short Stories
9789390575060	George Orwell Collected Works
9789390575077	George Orwell Essays
9789390575213	George Orwell Poems
9788194914150	Greatest Poetry Ever Written Vol 1
9788194914143	Greatest Poetry Ever Written Vol 1
9789390896301	Gulliver's Travel
9789390575961	Gunaho Ka Devta
9789390575893	H. P. Lovecraft Selected Stories Vol 1
9789390575978	H. P. Lovecraft Selected Stories Vol 2
9789390896059	Hamlet
9789390575022	His Last Bow: Some Reminiscences of Sherlock Holmes
9789390896134	History of Western Philosophy
9789390575121	Homage To Catalonia

9789390896219	How to develop self-confidence and Improve public Speaking
9789390896295	How to enjoy your life and your Job
9789390575633	How to own your own mind
9789390896318	How to read Human Nature
9789390896325	How to sell your way through the life
9789390896370	How to use the laws of mind
9789390896387	How to use the power of prayer
9789390896028	How to win friends & Influence People
9788194824176	How To Win Friends and Influence People
9789390896103	Humility The Beauty of Holiness
9789390896653	Imperialism the Highest Stage of Capitalism
9789390575084	In Our Time
9789390575169	In Our Time & Three Stories and Ten poems
9789390575145	James Allen: The Collected Works
9789390896189	Jesus Himself
9789390575480	Jo's Boys
9789390896394	Julius Caesar
9789390575404	Keep the Aspidistra Flying
9789390896400	Kidnapped
9789390896424	King Lear
9789390575824	Lady Susan
9789390896455	Law of Success
9789390896264	Lincoln The Unknown
9789390575565	Little Men
9789390575640	Little Women
9788194914174	Lost Horizon
9789390896462	Macbeth
9789390896929	Man Eaters of Kumaon
9789390896523	Man The Dwelling Place of God
9789390896349	Man The Dwelling Place of God
9789390575909	Mansfield Park
9788194914136	Manto Ki 25 Sarvshreshth Kahaniya
9789390896509	Marxism, Anarchism, Communism
9789390575664	Mathematical Principles of Natural Philosophy

9788194914198	Meditations
9789390575800	Mein Kampf
9789390575794	Memory How To Develop, Train, And Use It
9789390896486	Mind Power
9789390896585	Money
9789390575039	Mortal Coils
9789390575770	My Life and Work
9789390896035	Narrative of the Life of Frederick Douglass
9789390575152	Neville Goddard: The Collected Works
9789390575985	Northanger Abbey
9789390896530	Notes From Underground
9789390896547	Oliver Twist
9789390575459	On War
9789390575541	One, None and a Hundred Thousand
9789390896554	Othelo
9789390575435	Out Of This World
9789390575015	Persuasion
9789390575510	Prayer The Art Of Believing
9789390575091	Pride and Prejudice
9789390896561	Psychic Perception
9789390575381	Rabindranath Tagore - 5 Best Short Stories Vol 2
9789390575367	Rabindranath Tagore - Short Stories (Masters Collections Including The Childs Return)
9789390575374	Rabindranath Tagore 5 Best Short Stories Vol 1 (Including The Childs Return
9789390896622	Romeo & Juliet
9789390896127	Sanatana Dharma
9789390575596	Seedtime & Harvest
9789390896639	Selected Stories of Guy De Maupassant
9789390575206	Self-Reliance & Other Essays
9789390575176	Sense and Sensibility
9789390575299	Shyamchi Aai
9789390896738	Socialism Utopian and Scientific
9789390896646	Success Through a Positive Mental Attitude
9789390575428	The Adventures of Huckleberry Finn

9789390575183	The Adventures of Sherlock Holmes
9789390575343	The Adventures of Tom Sawyer
9789390896691	The Alchemy Of Happiness
9789390575862	The Art Of Public Speaking
9789390896288	The Autobiography Of Charles Darwin
9788194914181	The Best of Franz Kafka: The Metamorphosis & The Trial
9789390575008	The Call Of Cthulhu and Other Weird Tales
9789390575107	The Case-Book of Sherlock Holmes
9789390896110	The Castle Of Otranto
9789390896745	The Communist Manifesto
9789390575589	The Complete Fiction of H. P. Lovecraft
9789390575497	The Complete Works of Florence Scovel Shinn
9789390896820	The Conquest of Breard
9789390896813	The Diary of a Young Girl
9789390896332	The Diary of a Young Girl The Definitive Edition of the Worlds Most Famous Diary
9789390575701	The Great Gatsby, Animal Farm & 1984 (3In1)
9789390575312	The Greatest Works Of George Orwell (5 Books) Including 1984 & Non-Fiction
9789390575992	The Hound of Baskervilles
9789390896707	The Idiot
9789390896714	The Invisible Man
9789390575657	The Knowledge of the holy
9789390575558	The Law & the Promise
9789390896721	The Law Of Attraction
9789390896776	The Leader in you
9789390896363	The Life of Christ
9789390896196	The Man-Eating Leopard of Rudraprayag
9789390896783	The Master Key to Riches
9789390575268	The Memoirs Of Sherlock Holmes
9789390896479	The Midsummer Night's Dream
9789390575466	The Mill On The Floss
9789390896790	The Miracles of your mind
9789390896660	The Mutual Aid A Factor in Evolution
9789390896448	The Origin of Species

9789390896905	The Peter Kropotkin Anthology The Conquest of Bread & Mutual Aid A Factor of Evolution
9789390896806	The Picture of Dorian Gray
9789390896271	The Picture of Dorian Gray
9789390575275	The Power Of Awareness
9789390896356	The Power of Concentration
9788194824169	The Power of Positive Thinking
9789390575411	The Power of the Spoken Word
9788194914105	The Power Of Your Subconscious Mind
9789390896899	The Power of Your Subconscious Mind
9789390896417	The Principles of Communism
9789390575787	The Psychology Of Mans Possible Evolution
9789390896615	The Psychology of Salesmanship
9789390575732	The Pursuit of God
9789390575398	The Pursuit of Happiness
9789390896851	The Quick and Easy Way to effective Speaking
9789390575947	The Return Of Sherlock Holmes
9789390575138	The Road To Wigan Pier
9789390896981	The Root of the Righteous
9789390575855	The Science Of Being Well
9788194914167	The Science Of Getting Rich, The Science Of Being Great & The Science Of Being Well (3In1)
9789390896011	The Screwtape Letters
9789390896073	The Screwtape Letters
9789390575336	The Secret Door to Success
9789390575695	The Secret Of Imagining
9789390896868	The Secret Of Success
9789390896431	The Seven Last Words
9789390575930	The Sign of the Four
9789390896004	The Sonnets
9789390896516	The Souls of Black Folk
9789390896875	The Sound and The Fury
9789390575244	The State and Revolution
9789390896882	The Story of My Life
9789390896936	The Story Of Oriental Philosophy

9789390896752	The Strange Case of Dr. Jekyll and Mr. Hyde
9789390896943	The Tempest
9789390575916	The Valley Of Fear
9789390575879	The Wind in the willows
9789390896080	The Wind in the willows
9789390575763	Their eyes were watching gofd
9789390575831	Three Stories
9789390896950	Twelfth Night
9789390896592	Twelve Years a Slave
9789390896677	Up from Slavery
9789390896974	Value Price and Profit
9789390896967	Wake Up and Live
9789390896493	With Christ in the School of Prayer
9789390575602	Your Faith is Your Fortune
9789390575473	Your Infinite Power To Be Rich
9789390575251	Your Word is Your Wand
9789390575718	Youth
9789391316099	A Christmas Carol
9789391316105	A Doll's House
9789391316501	A Passage to India
9789391316709	A Portrait of the Artist as a Young Man
9789391316112	A Tale of Two Cities
9789391316747	A Tear and a Smile
9789391316167	Agnes Gray
9789391316174	Alice's Adventures in Wonderland
9789391316136	Anandamath
9789391316181	Anne Of Green Gables
9789391316754	Anthem
9789391316198	Around The World in 80 Days
9789391316013	As A Man Thinketh
9789391316242	Autobiography of a Yogi
9789391316266	Beyond Good and Evil
9789391316761	Bleak House
9789391316778	Chitra, a Play in One Act
9789391316310	David Copperfield

9789391316075	Demian
9789391316785	Dubliners
9789391316051	Favourite Tales from the Arabian Nights
9789391316235	Gitanjali
9789391316068	Gravity
9789391316150	Great Speeches of Abraham Lincoln
9789391316662	Guerilla Warfare
9789391316839	Kim
9789391316822	Mother
9789391316211	My Childhood
9789391316846	Nationalism
9789391316327	Oliver Twist
9789391316853	Pygmalion
9789391316334	Relativity: The Special and the General Theory
9789391316389	Scientific Healing Affirmation
9789391316341	Sons and Lovers
9789391316587	Tales from India
9789391316372	Tess of The D'Urbervilles
9789391316396	The Awakening and Selected Stories
9789391316402	The Bhagvad Gita
9789391316303	The Book of Enoch
9789391316228	The Canterville Ghost
9789391316907	The Dynamic Laws of Prosperity
9789391316006	The Great Gatsby
9789391316860	The Hungry Stones and Other Stories
9789391316433	The Idiot
9789391316440	The Importance of Being Earnest
9789391316297	The Light of Asia
9789391316914	The Madman His Parables and Poems
9789391316457	The Odyssey
9789391316921	The Picture of Dorian Gray
9789391316464	The Prince
9789391316938	The Prophet
9789391316945	The Republic
9789391316518	The Scarlet Letter

9789391316143	The Seven Laws of Teaching
9789391316525	The Story of My Experiments with Truth
9789391316532	The Tales of the Mother Goose
9789391316549	The Thirty Nine Steps
9789391316594	The Time Machine
9789391316600	The Turn of the Screw
9789391316983	The Upanishads
9789391316617	The Yellow Wallpaper
9789391316426	The Yoga Sutras of Patanjali
9789391316990	Ulysses
9789391316624	Utopia
9789391316679	Vanity Fair
9789391316020	What Is To Be Done
9789391316686	Within A Budding Grove
9789391316693	Women in Love